W9-BLT-783

FALLING IN LOVE
FOR ALL THE RIGHT REASONS

FALLING IN
LOVE
FOR ALL THE
RIGHT REASONS

HOW TO FIND YOUR SOUL MATE

Dr. Neil Clark Warren
with Ken Abraham

**CENTER
STREET**

NEW YORK   BOSTON   NASHVILLE

If you purchase this book without a cover you should be aware that this book may have been stolen property and reported as "unsold and destroyed" to the publisher. In such case neither the author nor the publisher has received any payment for this "stripped book."

Copyright © 2005 by eHarmony.com

All rights reserved. No part of this book may be reproduced in any form or by any electronic or mechanical means, including information storage and retrieval systems, without permission in writing from the publisher, except by a reviewer who may quote brief passages in a review.

Center Street

Time Warner Book Group
1271 Avenue of the Americas, New York, NY 10020
Visit our Web site at www.twbookmark.com

Center Street and the Center Street logo are trademarks of Time Warner Book Group Inc.

Printed in the United States of America
Originally published in hardcover by Center Street
First Trade Edition: December 2005
10 9 8 7 6 5 4 3 2 1

The Library of Congress has cataloged the hardcover edition as follows:
Warren, Neil Clark.
    Falling in love for all the right reasons : how to find your soul mate / Neil Clark Warren with Ken Abraham.
        p. cm.
    ISBN 0-446-57685-9
    1. Marriage. 2. Mate selection. 3. Dating (Social customs) 4. Love. I. Abraham, Ken. II. Title.
    HQ734.W31745 2005
    646.7'7—dc22   2004019845

ISBN: 0-446-69388-X (pbk.)

Cover Art by Caroline Woodham/Getty

To the thousands of couples who have been matched by eHarmony for all the right reasons . . . especially to those who have gotten married as a result of meeting on eHarmony.com . . .

And to all the couples in the future who will utilize the principles within these pages to set themselves up for marital happiness by making sure they have broad-based compatibility.

ACKNOWLEDGMENTS

Producing a book of this nature requires the concerted efforts of a number of highly skilled individuals, and I am deeply appreciative of their commitment to the task and their belief in the value of the effort. Certainly, more people contributed to the information in this book than I can possibly list here, but a few who merit special mention are:

Rolf Zettersten, my publisher on this adventure, and my friend. Thank you for encouraging me to pursue this project when it would have been easier to let go of it.

Ken Abraham, my collaborator on this book, an extremely talented writer, and more important, a wonderful man.

Greg Forgatch, the chief executive officer of eHarmony, and a virtual fountain of energy and ideas, with a commitment to take these principles to every single person in the world!

Joe Zink, Steve Carter, Galen Buckwalter, Greg Steiner, and Grant Langston. Thanks for sharing your insights with Ken and me as we worked on this book.

Sue Braden, the "rock" of eHarmony, my marvelous and dedicated administrative assistant who keeps us all on the same page.

Most of all, to Marylyn, my wife of more than forty-five years. Thank you for your unwavering commitment to excellence in all that we do, and for loving me so completely and unconditionally.

Thanks again to all the couples who have contributed to my thinking about what it takes to make a strong, successful marriage.

And special thanks to the more than one-hundred-thirty members of the eHarmony staff who contribute every day to an extension of our understanding of the principles that differentiate disappointing relationships from great marriages.

CONTENTS

G R O U P   3

Skills That Can Be Developed   161

G R O U P   4

Qualities That Can Be Developed   185

Matchmaker, Matchmaker

SINCE FORMING eHarmony in August 2000, I have been approached in the most unusual places by people with requests for help in finding lifelong love and happiness for themselves or someone they care about deeply. For instance, last year I was assisting in the wedding ceremony for a good friend, Elizabeth Nelson, when John Harris—a popular media correspondent—clutched my arm. I had known John for a number of years, but I was surprised nonetheless at the sense of urgency with which he sought me out.

"Neil, I have a daughter named Lauren," John said furtively. "She went through a divorce several years ago, and she's a wonderful young woman. She's bright, beautiful, and articulate." John paused and took a deep breath before continuing. "She has three great kids, so following the divorce, she moved back home and my wife and I have helped raise the children."

My friend stepped closer to me and lowered his voice. "But I have to tell you, she has not been able to find the right kind of person . . . not even to date, much less to marry. I've heard your advertisements on the radio, and I think she'd be a good candidate."

"Have her give me a call," I said, "and we'll see what we can do to help." I handed John a business card, feeling a bit awkward about holding our conversation in the midst of the bride and groom's receiving line, but wanting to assist nonetheless.

John later told me that while driving home after the wedding, he informed his wife, Janice, of our conversation: "I talked to Neil Warren about Lauren—"

Janice interrupted him. "Oh, John. You didn't! That's terrible. Have you lost your senses? You should never have done that! Lauren would *not* be happy. She would probably take that as an insult or be terribly embarrassed."

"Okay, fine," John said. "I'm sorry I mentioned it." He handed my business card to his wife. "No harm done."

About a month later, Lauren and her mother were engaged in a conversation concerning Lauren's stagnant social life. When Lauren mentioned her frustration at not being able to find a man with whom she felt strongly compatible, Janice let it slip that John had discussed her discouragement with me. "You know, your dad talked to Neil Warren about you at Elizabeth Nelson's wedding, and Neil gave him his business card for eHarmony . . . Let's see, I have it right here in my purse . . . but I told your father that you would not be the least bit interested . . ."

"Give me the card," Lauren said.

"Wha—?"

"Just give me the card," Lauren said.

Her mother found the card in her purse and handed it over to Lauren. She called me, and I explained to her how eHarmony.com works.

"I think I'd like to try that," Lauren said. She completed the eHarmony personality profile and eventually was matched with a man named Brian, a restorative architect who was also divorced and was raising two daughters by himself.

They began to communicate through the eHarmony Web site and quickly progressed through the four stages of "safe" correspondence leading to open communication. Before long, Lauren and Brian met and went out on a date. During their conversation, they couldn't believe how compatible they were. They shared common interests, values, and goals. They hit it off so well that they were finishing each other's sentences!

Within a year, Brian proposed to Lauren and the couple sent my wife, Marylyn, and me an invitation to their wedding. We're not able to attend many of the weddings of people who have met on the eHarmony Web site (we have been the first step down the aisle for more than six thousand marriages in the past few years!), but this was one wedding we didn't want to miss.

Lauren and Brian involved all five of their children—her three and his two—in the wedding ceremony, and it was truly the uniting of two families, not merely the marriage of two individuals in love. Prior to the service, Brian's sister introduced herself to me and said, "Thank you so much for bringing Lauren and Brian together." Tears welled in her eyes as she said, "I feel as though I've gotten my brother back. He has been lonely for such a long time and now he is so happy. I can't ever begin to thank you."

At the reception, when Marylyn and I greeted the bride and groom, Brian hugged me. I mean, he *hugged* me!

Brian is a strong man, and when he threw his arms around me, I knew I wasn't going anywhere; my arms instinctively went around his back. He said, "Neil Warren!" and he hugged me some more! I stood there awkwardly for a moment, and Brian continued to hang on to me. I let go of Brian and dropped my arms to my sides, the universal sign between males indicating "Okay, this hug is over," but Brian still kept me in his grip. Almost reluctantly, I lifted my arms back up around Brian's back and I hugged him a little bit longer. And he still held on to me! Three times I lowered and raised my arms, but Brian continued to cling to me. He hugged me for about a minute or a minute and a half, which seemed like forever with other people standing behind us waiting to greet the beaming bride and groom.

But Brian didn't care. "Thank you, Dr. Warren," he said over and over. "Lauren and I are so happy! We are so well matched. Thank you for bringing us together."

With more than six million people now using our Web site—and that number rising by more than ten thousand every day—eHarmony has brought together literally thousands of men and women—serious singles who are not simply looking for a date for Saturday night, but who are sincerely searching for lifelong marital success.

We have thousands of exciting stories in our eHarmony files—each one interesting and unique, yet all bearing witness to a strikingly simple and similar truth: When you discover a person with whom you have broad-based compatibility, your chances of experiencing true, lasting marital happiness rise exponentially.

But what is broad-based compatibility, and how can you find such a person with whom you may share it?

How will you know him or her when you meet? How can you be sure the person to whom you are initially attracted won't change into a stranger after the two of you have tied the marital knot? Even though you both enjoy sushi, or jogging at sunrise, will you still be in love twenty years from now? How can you avoid wasting years of time, enduring one painful relationship after another or—perhaps worse yet in your estimation—having no promising relationships at all?

In *Falling in Love for All the Right Reasons* you will discover the answers to these questions and many more that come to mind—or should—every time you consider a dating relationship with somebody of the opposite sex.

Nowadays, people tend to fall in love for all the wrong reasons. Physical appearance, power, prestige, social status, wealth, and sexual "chemistry" are a few of the more transient, fickle qualities on which men and women sometimes base their relationships. Not that those aspects of a relationship are unimportant. Indeed, they merit close examination and we will evaluate them in these pages, but they are not a sufficient foundation on which to build a solid, long-term marriage.

At eHarmony, we want you to fall in love for all the right reasons so you can remain in love for a lifetime. And because we have discovered twenty-nine dimensions that determine long-term success in marriage—scientifically proven principles of compatibility, based on more than thirty-eight years of research into what ingredients are required in a healthy, happy marriage—we feel absolutely confident that we can help you (or other singles you know) find "Mr. or Ms. Right." Even more important, we can help you establish a growing relationship with that person that potentially will lead to a successful marriage.

That's what *Falling in Love for All the Right Reasons* is all about. The good news is that thanks to modern technology, you are more likely to discover your soul mate—that person with whom you share the most "broad-based compatibility"—than ever before in the history of human relationships.

Think about that! You really do have a good chance of finding the love of your life! You can experience an incredible attraction, a thriving, fulfilling relationship that you will relish for a lifetime, and a magnificent marriage, all with a person who wants to share life at the deepest levels with someone such as you. Not only will this book help you to know yourself better and to know what sort of person you are looking for more specifically than you have ever imagined, but we'll even show you how you can best search for that person with whom you are most closely matched.

To boost your confidence, let me tell you a little about how eHarmony came together, how we developed these twenty-nine dimensions of compatibility, and how you can apply them and use them to evaluate a potential marriage relationship. Then we'll get extremely specific about what kind of person you should or should not marry.

Are you ready? This is going to be the adventure of your life!

FALLING IN LOVE
FOR ALL THE RIGHT REASONS

CHAPTER 1

How eHarmony Began

I CRINGED as I watched the couple leave my office after another hour-long session of counseling—an exercise in futility that left the three of us emotionally drained and as confused and frustrated as when we started. Ironically, Michelle and Robert weren't bad people; nor were they emotionally unhealthy people in desperate need of radical transformations in their thoughts, conversations, attitudes, or actions. Quite the contrary; they were both good people, caring and intelligent. They were simply two individuals traveling on parallel tracks in life that rarely intersected.

Worse yet, as much as I believe in the value of professional counseling and psychotherapy, I had to admit I was hard-pressed to help Michelle and Robert. Nor did I see any reason to refer them to another therapist for a second opinion. Passing them off to another counselor would merely cost the couple more money and exacerbate the problem. All I could really do for them was to encourage them to be kind to each other, forgiving, and to learn how to compromise, each one giving a little in the areas in which they were so utterly incompatible.

The truth is, Michelle and Robert should never have gotten married in the first place—at least, not to each other. As much as they sincerely tried to find common ground, they were horribly mismatched. They had known precious little warmth in their marriage since the early days, when the initial heat of their physical chemistry overshadowed their divergent interests. The fires of passion quickly cooled, however, in the year following their wedding. Their lack of compatibility naturally led to a lack of communication, which eventually took a toll on every part of their relationship. Lately they hadn't been fighting so much as ignoring each other. They lived in the same house but in different worlds.

As a psychotherapist for more than thirty-seven years, I have attempted to help thousands of couples grapple with marital problems of every conceivable sort. I have listened to men and women of various backgrounds and ages vent through their tears and anger about what went wrong in their marriages. In the process, I became increasingly convinced that we had to come up with a better system than traditional dating and mating; we had to find a better way for men and women to make a more accurate assessment of their potential compatibility *before* getting engaged or even deeply involved in a serious relationship. I came to believe that the key to revolutionizing marriage in North America was the matter of *selection*.

The state of marriage is downright alarming in the United States. Nine out of every ten people in the U.S. will marry at least once during their lifetime. But of the 90 percent of Americans who marry, 50 percent will divorce. Another 20 to 25 percent will remain married though miserable. Did you catch that awful statistic? Putting it bluntly, nearly 75 percent of the marriages that take place this year will eventually turn sour. *Seventy-five percent!* Worse yet, marital satisfaction is declining at a surprisingly rapid rate. Many couples start having serious troubles within a year after the wedding. Twenty percent of first marriages are over within five years. Thirty-three percent are over within ten years. Forty-three percent are over within fifteen years. And we know the failure rate goes to at least 50 percent. Now, of the 50 percent of those first marriages that stay together, nearly half of them will have at least one partner who admits, "I am not happy."

Many people will marry and divorce several times in their search for a truly satisfying relationship. Moreover, with every marital failure the chances of experiencing another divorce go up about 10 percent.

Something is terribly wrong!

The more I studied the matter, the more convinced I became that the overwhelming majority of failed marriages I encountered were in trouble on the day of the wedding. Quite simply, one or both members of the couple had chosen the wrong person to marry.

Does that seem blatantly obvious to you? Believe me, it is not nearly so apparent to thousands of couples who decide to marry every year. Many of them later admit that they did indeed feel reticence tugging at their hearts and minds on their wedding day, but they were too far down the road to turn back and halt the process.

"Something started churning inside me the moment the doors of the church sanctuary opened and I took that first step down the aisle," said Andrea, a twenty-eight-year-old who was terribly disappointed in her marriage. "It wasn't just the jitters. It was much more than that. I knew Kent and I had huge differences in our backgrounds, our attitudes toward family, and our goals in life, but we were in love and had dated for nearly two years. Marriage seemed like the next logical step for us. When I saw Kent and his groomsmen standing there at the front of the church, I knew the truth. Everything within me wanted to turn and run out of the building. But Mom and Dad had spent a small fortune on this wedding, and all our friends and family were there waiting for me to say, 'I do.' So I did. Now I wish that I hadn't."

Other couples all too soon learn the bad news that their relationship was based on insufficient compatibility. "I knew the first night of our honeymoon that our marriage was doomed," said Brandon, an extremely talented architect. "Not because we couldn't have great sex. We did! But as Beth and I basked in the supposed afterglow and I thought about spending the rest of my life with this woman, it hit me that great sex was nearly all we had in common."

From Beth's perspective, the physical relationship was a means of expressing her love for Brandon, and she was baffled at the eventual breakdown of their relationship. "I just don't understand," she said through her tears. "Brandon pursued me constantly before we were married, buying me nice things, taking me to fancy art galleries and other places I'd never been before. I knew I wasn't as smart as he is, but then nobody I know is. I felt that even though I wasn't able to grasp all his architect talk, we'd have no trouble communicating in other ways, especially in the bedroom. I guess I was mistaken."

Sadly so.

With the help of a competent counselor, Andrea and Kent were able to salvage their shaky marriage but, unfortunately, Brandon and Beth split up before they'd been married a year. Both couples were guilty of making poor choices when it came to picking a marriage partner.

How can you avoid making a similar mistake or making another mistake if you have already experienced a failed marriage? Throughout this book I'll give you dozens of ways to avoid such a calamity, but the starting place is to take the decision of marriage very seriously.

Over the years, as I've studied what ingredients go into making a great marriage, I've come to understand one of the foundational principles of life: Selecting the right person for marriage is the most underappreciated challenge in the human experience. My wife, Marylyn, and I were probably typical of many other couples in our dating days. We had almost no factually based understanding about what qualities were necessary for a good marriage. At the time Marylyn and I contemplated marriage, all I knew about her was that she was pretty and she made me feel good about myself. She also satisfied my extremely short list of requirements in a mate: I was taller than Marylyn; I was also older than she. She wasn't a member of my religious group—but she was willing to switch. (Actually, the fact that Marylyn wasn't tied in to my particular religious group made her more attractive to me. More about that later.)

I had no idea how talented she is; nor did I realize the amount of ambition she possesses or how incredibly intelligent she is, although I should have recognized that one. Marylyn's dad attended Massachusetts Institute of Technology and became an engineer. Marylyn was awarded the Most Outstanding Graduate trophy in her graduating class at Pepperdine University. Nevertheless, I didn't really understand how bright she is until much later. I didn't know her values. I had no idea how loyal she is. I knew little of her family background, especially the fact that she witnessed a miserable marriage relationship between her mother and father.

Despite my lack of understanding of the woman to whom I

wanted to commit my life, Marylyn and I got married . . . and we lucked out. We have an "A" marriage, and we've been happily married now for nearly half a century!

On the other hand, Marylyn and I have six extremely close friends. Four of those six individuals have each been married three times. They are all good people, well-intended, deeply spiritual, hardworking, and bright. They went into their marriages with all the hopes and dreams for success that Marylyn and I had enjoyed. But some of them married too early, broke up, and bounced out of the first marriage right into another. As I've often said, you can turn one bad marriage into two bad marriages so fast that it will make your head spin! That's what some of our friends did. Others divorced for various reasons. In still other cases, the second spouse died, which led to another marriage.

Somehow, Marylyn and I were spared that awful pain. How? Why? We don't know.

I was discussing this question with a highly respected psychologist who has been happily married for decades, and he offered a keen insight. "I, too, have often wondered what made the difference between our marriages," he said, "and those of some of our close friends from college who are divorced today. I'm convinced that you must pray passionately for a great marriage partner, and then you need to follow the rules."

That's good advice; unfortunately, I didn't know the rules! Marylyn and I didn't even know there were any rules regarding marriage, other than to be nice and try to get along. We were walking across thin ice in the middle of the night and we didn't even know it.

As I pondered marriages such as Michelle and Robert's, and Andrea and Kent's, Beth and Brandon's, and Marylyn's and mine, I became all the more determined to find a better way of matching couples.

In 1995 I moved my counseling practice to a new office in Pasadena. Much of my time was consumed with creating materials to teach people how they could have a better marriage. One day while talking with my son-in-law Greg Forgatch, I told him about a study I had done in which I asked one hundred married couples to tell me what makes a great marriage. Greg's eyes lit up as I talked about the information I had culled from the couples' responses.

The more we talked, the more we wondered about the possibility of creating a service for singles based on that kind of information.

We began to dream of an educational service based on the principles we had uncovered. We stewed on the idea, and the more we thought about it, the more excited we both became.

We were also motivated by the awful knowledge that 75 percent of first marriages end in divorce or unhappiness. We were determined to attempt to turn those figures around. Granted, in recent years the U.S. government has expressed the noble desire to help couples stay together, and has encouraged numerous beneficial premarital programs; many religious groups have placed a new emphasis on preparation for marriage as well, but much of the government and church emphasis on premarital counseling is too late.

Once an engagement ring goes on the finger, and a couple heads down the aisle, it is rare that they stop long enough to evaluate the merits or quality of their relationship. Any discomfort they feel is attributed to the stress of getting ready for the wedding. Actually, red flags may be flying all around them, but the couple often ignore them . . . until after they are married. A few months or years later, they find themselves ready to rip the marriage apart.

I hope the material in this book will help you to evaluate your potential mate for satisfaction in a marriage relationship long before you ever get to premarital counseling. I've seen far too many mismatched couples. My own mother and father were wonderful people, but less than spectacularly matched marriage partners. My dad was extremely bright and my mother was very sweet. Both were fine individuals; they just did not match each other very well in marriage, so there was little conversation or affection expressed between them around our home. They remained married for seventy years, but their relationship was anything but an ideal model of thoughtful marital matching. They were kind and considerate toward each other, but in essence they were not soul mates at all; they were more like coexisting roommates.

Greg and I began to dream big dreams of actually changing the fabric of society, one marriage at a time. Imagine that we could increase a couple's satisfaction with their marriage by 10 percent each year. Would they want to leave such a growing relationship? I doubt it. Better still, imagine that we could reduce the divorce rate by even 1 percent. That would affect the lives of nearly a million people in one generation. Now, imagine that we could do that each year by helping couples choose their mates much more wisely! Dare to really dream with us: Imagine that we could reduce the divorce rate 1 percent each year until it reaches single digits. This could represent the greatest social revolution in the history of the human race!

Impossible? Oh, no! All things are possible to the person who believes and is willing to work toward his or her goal. And Greg and I believed. We were certain we could make some real progress in combating one of North America's most debilitating social problems.

You Can't Be Serious!

Although I am a passionate dreamer, I could never have imagined the possibility of matching two people for such a serious relationship as marriage . . . on the *Internet*, of all places!

But in 1997 Greg and I traveled to Santa Monica, California, where we met Pete Hart, the former CEO of MasterCard and the eventual CEO of Advanta (a financial services company for small businesses). Pete and Greg "clicked" right away and I, too, was intrigued by the personable, intelligent Hart. Visionary that he is, Pete was one of the first people to see the potential of widespread matchmaking. Years before, he had convinced his company to acquire an existing dating service. Unfortunately, after pumping millions of dollars into the business, it simply failed to work as Pete had hoped. But he never lost enthusiasm for his vision.

Out of that experience, however, Pete became convinced that the only way a matchmaking company could succeed was to expand the pool of available partners and develop a rigorous matching model. And the most hopeful way of doing that seemed to be by means of the Internet.

Pete passionately encouraged Greg and me to develop a model

program and put it on the Internet market as soon as possible. "I'll be your adviser," he said, "but only if you will use the Internet." The Harvard-trained business leader reminded us: "In every business, success goes to the person who gets to the market first. The first person to the market has an enormous advantage. Just get your product together and get it out there. You can refine it as you go."

Greg respectfully disagreed with Pete's advice. He gently protested, "That works well when you're selling vacuum cleaners—I'll make it better next time, getting into the corners, getting into the woof of the carpet without pulling it off the floor—or some other sort of product, but these are people's lives we're talking about. We don't dare put our 'product' on the market with a disclaimer saying, 'Hey everybody, we think this is a pretty good plan, but it's the early version, so we're not totally sure you can trust it. But don't worry; we'll make the next version better.'" Greg looked at me and said, "Neil, if we are going to put your name on it, and you are going to speak to the public about it, our product has to work. You have to be able to believe in it."

I agreed with Greg wholeheartedly. Consequently, we took another year and a half to gather and reanalyze our empirical data. The more information we collected and studied, the more clearly our twenty-nine dimensions slowly but surely began to crystallize and surface. It was well worth the extra effort, but it wasn't easy.

Before we went online, Greg and I wanted to discover what qualities made a marriage work well—not simply survive, but thrive. To collect accurate, reliable information, we decided to devise a questionnaire for married couples to complete. We developed a team of researchers comprised of PhDs and research assistants, many of whom had worked alongside me when I taught graduate-level psychology classes. Dr. Galen Buckwalter, a brilliant former student of mine, was one of the first to come on board after Greg Forgatch.

Galen was a story in himself. He had suffered a severe diving accident as a teenager that left him a quadriplegic. He could not walk and had great difficulty using his arms and fingers. He typed by grasping two pencils in his hands and using the eraser ends to tap the keyboard. Although his body often worked against him, Galen's mind was amazing and his determination to overcome his injury was downright inspiring. He has written hundreds of articles for major psychological publications, and he even performs in a "rock" band— all from a wheelchair!

Each morning, after taking three hours to get ready, Galen came to my office and worked on the questions for our "model," the form we wanted to use as our survey of married couples. Galen introduced us to his friend Steve Carter, who was taking a break from his doctoral program for a while and was fascinated by the scientific study of the factors that made for a good marriage relationship. Steve joined us in our quest. Soon Steve brought in another friend, Grant Langston, and we started meeting every day, working on questions we wanted to ask married couples. Many of the questions revolved loosely around the ten keys to a successful relationship I had presented in my book *Finding the Love of Your Life*. That's where we started, but with the brilliant minds involved in the research process, we soon far surpassed those ten areas and began devising questions I'd never even considered. Many others spun off wildly in all directions, but we always came back to that one basic issue: What does it take to make a marriage succeed?

A business associate of Greg's, Kevin Burke, also assisted us greatly in the process. Kevin is the director of Lucid Marketing, a company with great expertise in customer relations. It was Kevin who first almost whimsically tagged our fledgling company and future Internet site with the name "eHarmony.com." It was a stroke of genius, as the name implies what we are all about—bringing true harmony into the lives of the couples we match online.

Sweet, syrupy sentiments aside, I must admit that I wasn't a big fan of the name at first. It didn't snap like Match.com. But since we were merely planning to use it on the questionnaire we were sending out to gather information from married couples, I felt I could live with it. However, the response to the name and the questionnaire was overwhelming. More than five thousand questionnaires were returned to eHarmony, and we used nearly a thousand couples as our first test group. The name grew on me and now I'm glad we chose it. In fact, eHarmony.com was the first and only name we considered; the company has never had any other moniker.

In recent years, we have developed and updated numerous versions of that first battery of questions and received valuable information from hundreds of marriages. Beyond that, I did "divorce autopsies" on 512 failed marriages. I wanted to discover what caused the marital breakups. Were there any common threads, any recurring "marriage killers" that other couples could avoid? Combining this information with the insights we garnered from the first test groups, we were able to discern accurately similar qualities that colored every great marriage, while noting potential problems that could plunge mismatched couples into disillusionment, despair, and even divorce. We could also predict where the land mines might be hidden, lying in wait for even solid, well-matched, forward-moving relationships.

As we analyzed the feedback from these five thousand couples, we categorized them according to their levels of marriage satisfaction. We kept it relatively simple at first, putting the responses into four groups: those of very happily married people; those who were moderately happy; those who were fairly unhappy; and those who were terribly disappointed with their marriages.

With Galen and Steve leading us, we spent hundreds of hours looking carefully at the differences between the number one group, the very happily married people, and the number four group, the very disappointed group. As we studied the information, we discovered that there were not simply two or three major differences; there were, in fact, twenty-nine dimensions on which the very happily married couples were extremely well matched. Similarly, we discovered that when couples were poorly matched on those same twenty-nine dimensions, they inevitably were most unhappily married.

Clearly, if you get these twenty-nine dimensions well matched, you are on your way to a lifetime of great marital success. If you get good at recognizing these twenty-nine dimensions and learn to discern when you are well matched, you will know specifically how to find the best partner, develop a fantastic relationship, and maintain a great marriage.

Interestingly, the data we gleaned from the research mirrored almost identically the conclusions I had drawn clinically from my years as a psychotherapist and counselor. Our research team went back to work and developed what eventually became a 436-question survey that would produce an accurate personality profile of any person we wanted to match with a potential mate. This was a key ingredient to eHarmony. Thanks to the scientific research we conducted, we were also able to build into the questionnaire several preventive screens to help alert us to people we could not match well. Unlike existing online dating services, we wanted to provide singles searching for a serious, potentially long-term relationship with more than a picture and a brief paragraph of biographical information about the people they might like to meet. Our questionnaire was not designed to merely hook people up for dates, although that was a natural result. More so, it was designed to identify a person's core characteristics, beliefs, values, emotional health, and relationship skills.

We quickly discovered that the length of our questionnaire did not deter serious, marriage-minded singles. In fact, the sheer size of the questionnaire did several positive things for us. First, it provided a wealth of information on which we could base our matches; second, it alerted us to people looking merely for a fling and other wounded people who sometimes look to Internet matchmaking services as a pool in which they can troll. Most important, the mass of questions automatically filtered out many who were not interested in pursuing a serious relationship that could culminate in marriage. Someone just looking for a date on Saturday night would not usually be willing to spend the time and effort to complete the huge questionnaire. Other Internet sites provide quick "get a date" services; eHarmony does not.

Still today, our daunting questionnaire does not prove to be too overwhelming for most serious-minded people who visit the site. Approximately three out of four of the people who begin the questionnaire complete it (some actually leave it for a while and return to finish it). We found two main reasons for this phenomenon: One, people love to learn about themselves; and two, they realize that by providing as much accurate information as possible they enhance the possibility of being matched well.

We decided to offer a personality profile based on the information provided in our questionnaire—normally a $40 value—free of charge to anyone who took the time to complete the long inventory on eHarmony.com. After hundreds of hours of working together to create a psychologically and mathematically sound matching system, we were ready to go online.

Technically, we were ready. Emotionally, I still had occasional misgivings. Although Greg and I recognized the enormous potential represented by the Internet, in my doubtful moments, the very idea of starting an Internet matchmaking company seemed a bit tacky. I had spent my entire life in academic circles. Was I now going to lower myself to hawking advice online?

Questions abounded concerning Internet matching and dating. Why would anyone want to go on the Internet in search of a marriage partner? Isn't the Internet risky and dangerous? Aren't pornography and perversion rampant on the Internet? Could I really encourage my friends or family members to visit a matchmaking site?

Then there were the stigmas to consider: Aren't Internet matchmaking services only for "losers," people who couldn't meet someone or get a date any other way? Isn't physical attraction, that indefinable element of "chemistry," the most important element in a relationship? So how can you actually match for that? And what about the many parents and friends who think Internet matching is dangerous, unsophisticated, or worse?

These misconceptions had to be overcome in our own hearts and minds first before we could launch a matchmaking site in good conscience.

Admittedly, we had discovered through our research that many so-called matchmaking services were nothing more than moneymaking machines. One former sales representative for such a company explained to us why he quit. "I used to look out in my lobby," he said, "and it would be filled with needy men and women. I'd interview the one I considered the most needy, because that was the person I assumed I could sell most easily on our program. Once behind the closed doors of my office, I'd question her thoroughly for the next half hour, basically recounting how horribly ineffective she had been with the opposite sex. Throughout the process, I subtly beat up on her self-esteem.

"Then I'd offer her all sorts of false hope about the prospective dates we were going to arrange for her. I'd tell her, 'Now, Thelma, when I get you a date Thursday night, and another date on Friday night, if I call you on Saturday afternoon, telling you that we have another date for you on Saturday night, you can't tell me that you are too tired.'

"Of course, Thelma hasn't been on a date in three and a half years, so the very thought of going out three times in one weekend is almost more than her throbbing heart can stand. She signs on the dotted line.

"At that point, it is a piece of cake to 'up-sell' her everything we have in our bag of tricks, and she walks out with a thousand-dollar membership, or maybe even a five-thousand-dollar membership. The goal is similar to selling health club memberships, to collect as much cash as we can up front and hope that the clients never show up again. I finally quit the job when I couldn't stand to look myself in the mirror anymore."

As we researched the competition, we also discovered that most online dating services are basically picture-browsing smorgasbords, including thousands of photos of potential dates, along with some basic biographical information such as their occupation, favorite movies and music, and some of their favorite things to do. That's not necessarily bad; it just isn't enough. Seeing someone's photo and bio doesn't necessarily do anything to help improve the odds of success in choosing a marriage partner. On the other hand, the photos do provide individuals an opportunity to see potential partners who are out there, people they may never otherwise see.

Ted, a thirty-three-year-old single dad, found the picture-browsing sites to be encouraging. "I don't have time to date a lot," he said, "so I sure don't have time to date people to whom I am not physically attracted. Sorting through the photographs helps me see who I am *not* interested in."

With our program, we decided that we wanted to do something different; we wanted couples to fall in love from the inside out, to fall in love with the *person*, not simply with his or her appearance, what he or she did for a living, or what he or she possessed. We felt certain that if couples could fall in love on this basis, the relationship would have a much better chance of survival. With that in mind, we reached a landmark decision: We would encourage our clients to resist exchanging photographs of themselves on the Web site for as long as possible. We recognized the natural inclination to want to see the other person with whom you are communicating by means of e-mail, but we urged people to resist that temptation, at least until they were well along in the initial stages of communication. We believed—and still do—that if people could fall in love with the inner person, the external appearance would not be as great a factor. Indeed, some less attractive people may actually appear better looking once you've gotten to know his or her "heart."

When Greg told his wife, Lorrie, that we were going to start a matchmaking company, she looked around their kitchen in despair. "We're gone. We're going to lose everything we own," she groaned. "This isn't going to work."

But when Greg informed Lorrie that we were not going to match individuals on external appearances or bank accounts, but on values, character, and other inner qualities, she caught the vision for what we could do. "Okay, I can see that. People will buy that."

As we began developing our eHarmony team, we didn't go to other Internet companies in an attempt to hire away their best people. That would have produced an environment of MBAs, marketing people, and Internet techies who said, "Well, the last five times we created one of these Internet companies, we did it this way."

Greg and I weren't all that interested in what other Internet companies had done. We wanted highly qualified people who could tap into our vision to quell the escalating divorce rates and to improve the quality of marriage in America and around the world. Although I approached the problem from a faith-based, Christian worldview, we have people of numerous ethnic backgrounds, races, and religious faiths harmoniously working together at eHarmony. The common denominator about our people is that they all really "get it." They see the potential for eHarmony to positively change the fabric of marriages around the world.

Greg Forgatch, the CEO of eHarmony, often quips that the company was started by a "shrink, a trucker, and a real estate broker." Obviously, I'm the "shrink"; Greg Steiner, our chief operations officer (who has been with us since eHarmony launched and is, in my opinion, the best COO of any business in North America), has a background in the freight transportation industry, so he knows how to deliver a product and maintain quality controls; and Greg Forgatch came to us out of the real estate business and is one of the most conscientious sales and marketing guys I've ever known.

Added to that mix is my wife, Marylyn, who is brighter than all of us in many respects and has a background in fund-raising. Working for the world-famous Huntington Library in San Marino, near Pasadena, Marylyn raised more than $150 million during her tenure as a library executive. From the beginning of eHarmony, Marylyn has been our best public relations person; she truly believes in the concept of finding a person the love of his or her life.

We had a good team, with people to lead the psychological and creative aspects, the sales of our services, and the delivery system to get the product to market. Still, nobody on our developmental team had any real assurance that our idea would actually work. We had secured a few financial grants to help get us started and had lined up investors to help us afford the initial launch costs. The equipment and technology alone for the eHarmony.com Web site consumed a high percentage of our total capitalization of $3.1 million. And we had no users!

Worse yet, we didn't have the luxury of many start-up businesses that could grow slowly. For eHarmony to work well, we needed lots of people to come online quickly.

They didn't.

Despite our massive research and our elaborate matching system, eHarmony.com was slow to catch on with the public. Consequently, our "pool" of people seeking to be matched was simply too small to do a good job for them. We kept our prices reasonable, while cutting our budget extremely close to the bone.

I remember the stark terror I felt when "Kathy," our first woman who wanted to be matched, signed on to eHarmony. *Who in the world are we going to match her with?* I fretted. We didn't have enough men on the site yet. Of course, before long we had a few thousand singles on the site, then several hundred thousand people on the site, and that problem took care of itself.

Still, it was rough going at first. Today, we have had over six million people register online, and we are adding nearly ten thousand new people every day! Thousands of matches have been made on eHarmony, resulting in more than six thousand marriages so far. Now, we hear about five to ten weddings and twenty or more serious relationships *every day* in which the couples have been matched by eHarmony. But it didn't happen overnight, and eHarmony almost didn't happen at all! From August 2000 to December 2000, we struggled every day just to stay in business.

I had closed my practice as a clinical psychologist and therapist so I could devote myself full-time to speaking about and promoting eHarmony. I appeared on every radio and television show that would give me a few minutes to talk about our venture. Marylyn and I traveled extensively, trying to convince the media, singles groups, and especially leaders of singles groups, of the benefits and potential value of encouraging their constituencies to join eHarmony. Only a few caught the vision. Meanwhile, our financial resources continued to dwindle.

We came extremely close to shutting down the site and giving up in despair and frustration. That's when I received an invitation to be a guest on a nationally syndicated radio talk show. The host knew about eHarmony and wanted to inform his audience about the potentials and the pitfalls of Internet dating sites. I knew that appearing on the show could be risky, since we were not really a "dating" site, but it was a chance we had to take.

Love Is in the Air

It snows early in Colorado, sometimes as soon as October, so I wasn't surprised when a brisk wind slapped me in the face as I exited the airport and headed for the radio studio on an early December morning. Once inside the studio, the warmth of the host and his staff was in direct contrast to the chilly air outside. I felt that I was among friends.

The host wanted to do a program aimed at those single adults who were looking for mates. He knew the subject of online matchmaking might be provocative, but he seemed sincerely interested and appeared to believe that his audience might benefit from the information I could provide.

We did the interview and it went well. I explained to the host that online dating services were a growing trend among single adults. Statistics showed that ninety-eight million Americans were single at the time and, according to American demographics, 22 percent of singles were actively looking for love online; 53 percent of those people claimed to be looking for a long-term commitment of marriage. That was the group eHarmony could really help. In the process of explaining eHarmony's intricate matching system, I explained that we wanted people to fall in love from the inside out, based on character, similarities, and values. I emphasized that we were not interested in merely getting somebody a date for the weekend, but we wanted to help find a single person his or her soul mate.

The moment I uttered the term "soul mate," it was as though an electric shock shot through the studio. I noticed the host's eyebrows rise in an expression of interest. Clearly, the phrase was one that resonated with him and his audience. Soul mate was a familiar term to me, one that I have used for years to describe a relationship between two people who are highly compatible. More recently, thanks to the enormous amount of data our eHarmony research team has been compiling about relationships, I've come to expand my definition even further. More about that later, but suffice it to say here that "soul mate" was a concept that meant much more to me than simply someone to be attracted to or frankly, even someone to marry. Unfortunately, I'd seen far too many marriage partners who were not soul mates. Genuine soul mates didn't merely have a few good things going for them; they had a *lot* of areas in which they were compatible. That message came out again and again on the radio program.

When I left the studio that day, I felt pleased about what we had accomplished. Besides demythologizing some of the stigmas of Internet matchmaking, I felt eHarmony had received some very positive publicity. I wondered if we would see any increase in the number of people checking us out online as a result of my participation in the show.

I was totally unprepared for the overwhelming, heartwarming response we received. Apparently, individuals all over the country were interested in finding a soul mate. "I'm tired of dinner and a movie," said one woman in her early thirties. "It's the same thing week after week. The only things that change are the menus and the movies. I want more. I want to find someone with whom I am compatible in a much broader way. I want to find my *soul mate*!"

Not only did we pick up new members to eHarmony following my interview on the nationally broadcasted radio show, we multiplied from barely 4,000 people on our site at the time to more than 350,000 singles on eHarmony within twenty-four months! The most gratifying aspect was the heartfelt responses we started receiving from the participants. Our matching system was working! We nearly went through the roof with excitement when we heard about the first marriage between two people who had met on eHarmony.com.

In 2002 I was invited to return to the nationally syndicated radio show to present an update. By then we were adding nearly one thousand new users every day and more than two hundred couples had married after being matched on eHarmony. The producers invited ten couples who had met on eHarmony to also take part in the interview. Nine of the couples had already gotten married and one couple was engaged to be married. One couple was pregnant with their first baby. Two couples were in their early twenties, two couples were in their thirties, two were in their forties, two couples were in their fifties, and two couples were beyond sixty years of age. I had met only one of these men and women prior to our invitation to be interviewed on the program.

The morning of the show I was privileged to spend a few minutes with the participants at our hotel. As the individuals shared with me their stories of how eHarmony had helped them find their soul mates, I was literally moved to tears. Suddenly, those long, tedious weeks and months of research and the enormous financial risks all seemed worthwhile.

When the host asked me to describe why we had started eHarmony and what made eHarmony different from other online matching sites, I was primed and ready. "There are nearly one hundred million singles in the United States, plus all the single men and women in Canada and in other countries that may hear this broadcast," I began. "Over 94 percent of them, pollster George Gallup discovered, want to marry their soul mate. Eighty-eight percent of them know it will take a lot of work to make it happen and 86 percent are willing to do the hard work to try to find that soul mate.

"Nevertheless, it is difficult to find a person who matches you in such a broad range of variables that you can say, 'Wow! I trust this person; he is my best friend; her intellect is a lot like mine; spiritually we are on the same wavelength. This person is similar to me in background, work ethic, ambition, energy, worldview, and values.' Finding that sort of person is a challenge, but most singles would love to meet such a match if possible. The problem, of course, is that if you are an average single man or woman, your circle of friends is too small to include more than a few potential dating relationships, and far fewer yet would come close to being a soul mate.

"That's where eHarmony can help. We can greatly increase your pool of potential singles from which to choose and we can match you with someone with whom you are compatible in twenty-nine crucial dimensions of a great relationship. We want people to fall in love with each other from the inside out. That is what we are trying to promote. We are fighting off, as much as we can, the powerful influence of a culture that purports that the only thing that matters in selecting a mate is how a person looks, or the kind of chemical turn-on you experience when you are near that person of the opposite sex, or how much money he or she makes. We are saying that the key factors in a good relationship are matters of the heart, the soul, the mind, the personality, the values, the spirituality of a person; matching these kinds of dimensions will make for a long-term, successful relationship."

We talked further about how eHarmony worked, and then the host proceeded to interview the couples who had met on eHarmony. I half held my breath in anticipation, not having any idea how they would respond. But I soon realized I had nothing to worry about. Far from it! The couples spoke of eHarmony in such glowing terms, I could feel the tears forming in my eyes all over again.

Jennifer and Jack lived about fifty miles from each other in Florida but had never met prior to being matched on eHarmony. "I became very discouraged about ever finding the right person to marry," said Jennifer. "It had gotten to the point that as a woman in my mid-thirties, I couldn't even attend weddings anymore. They were too painful to watch and listen to, too much of a reminder of my own loneliness. I had wedding dresses in my closet that were many different colors, but none of them were white.

"When I heard Dr. Warren on the radio in December, that first broadcast, I signed right up, and I received three matches almost immediately.

"Jack was my first match and then I had another. My second match, I could tell by the information given to me that he wasn't someone I wanted to pursue. So, I initiated the contact with Jack, and within a day he responded."

Jack picked up the story. "I had been married before and divorced and had been involved in a lot of singles groups. Because of that involvement, I set some standards for myself that I wouldn't drop. Consequently, I remained single for thirteen years following the divorce. I had gotten to the point that dating seemed like a waste. It just takes too much effort and too much of an investment of my time, risking my emotions, risking getting hurt or hurting someone else; establishing a new relationship, then six months down the road, realizing that I really don't want to spend the rest of my life with this person. I decided I would just stay single all my life.

"Then one day I was driving down the road and I heard the broadcast about eHarmony. I reached over on my mileage chart and wrote down the eHarmony Web site address. I went home that night and said, 'For a personality profile, free is my kind of price.'

"Little did I know, of course, that Jennifer had been listening to that same broadcast, and my true love of a lifetime was a mere fifty miles away. Had it not been for eHarmony, we most likely would never have met each other. If we had met in any other setting, we probably wouldn't have given each other the time of day. She just looked like too much work, too much effort. I didn't meet her standards, and I wasn't up to her expectations, so why bother? But through eHarmony, we both discovered that we not only met, but we surpassed our high standards!"

Becky and Tom were the engaged couple on the radio show that day. One of Becky's housemates—an editor of a single parents' magazine—came home from a conference with a six-minute video about eHarmony. She called her housemates together and said, "I want to see what you think about this."

Becky and her three friends sat down and watched the video. "We were pretty skeptical at first," said Becky. "What kind of loser goes to an Internet site to find his or her life mate? But by the end of the video, I had come to a point where I realized that this is a means that God could use to bring me together with a mate. It is not necessarily for everyone, but eHarmony could be a tool to bring people together. I signed on and fell in love with my very first match, Tom."

Tom had been even more skeptical than Becky. "My mom and dad heard that first broadcast in 2000 and told me about eHarmony," Tom recalled. "I didn't put a lot of stock in it. I didn't date much, because I live in a very small town. I went to church, and the church didn't have any people my age. A lot of people in my town had been divorced and had kids, and that's not what I really wanted in a relationship. If I got married, I wanted it to be our first marriage, our first house, and our first kids. Nothing against those people who have been married previously, but as a single guy who had never been married, those things were important to me; that is what I wanted. But in the small town in which I lived, there weren't too many women my age who fit into that category. My sister encouraged me to complete the eHarmony profile, so I went on and clicked 'Yes, find me a match.' But there was no match for me. That didn't help my loneliness. Here was this nationwide search, and there were no matches for me! But I waited and was patient, and a couple of weeks later, I got five matches.

Four of the women were not appealing to me. Then, I got matched with Rebecca. We've been going together now for fourteen months, and our wedding is right around the corner!"

Another couple, Emily and Jason Smith, had been married slightly over eight months and were already expecting their first baby. Emily's mother had heard the radio broadcast in December 2000 and had tucked the idea away in the back of her mind. In February, while visiting twenty-eight-year-old Emily in Denver, her mom picked up a book in which she had written "www.eHarmony.com." Seeing the Web site address jogged her memory, and she ordered a tape of the program for Emily. When Emily listened to the interview, it piqued her interest because, as she said later, "Dr. Warren explained so thoroughly the idea behind the Web site. It gave me enough confidence to go ahead and take the risk."

"I was skeptical and scared," admitted Emily, "but I trusted Dr. Warren because I had read *Finding the Love of Your Life*. I signed on, and Jason was actually my first match—actually, he was my one and only match!

"We wrote e-mail letters and journals for two months and eventually talked on the phone before we met in person. As we went through the process and we got to know each other, we realized that *this person was really matched up with me*. We both knew that we were the one for each other before we actually met in person."

Jason concurred. "We always tell everybody that our moms set us up, because I heard about the site from my mother also. She saw a television show on which Dr. Warren was a guest and she told me about it. I was living in Seattle at the time and Emily was living in Denver. When we started communicating, immediately we wanted to meet each other, within a couple of weeks. I am in the United States Coast Guard and I had to go out East for some training, so I scheduled my traveling to go through Colorado. We met each other in Denver in May 2001, and two days later I told her that she was the one for me. Within two weeks, we had our parents together and we told them that we wanted to get married. Within six months we were married and a month later we had a baby on the way!"

Jason had some further advice for singles, echoing some themes we'll look at later in this book. "You must have a passion to find the love of your life," he said, "to take the time and effort to work through that process in relationship building. If you meet someone at work, or somebody in church or school, and you don't take the time to know yourself, and you don't know what you want and don't know what kind of person you want to spend your life with, it's not going to work. But eHarmony is a tool that makes it easier, because the resources are right there for you."

I marveled at the way these young couples glowed with love as they told their stories. But I was even more amazed when some of the older members of the group—several of whom had been through heartrending breakups in their former marriages—began to share how hope had been rekindled in their hearts by eHarmony. Their stories nearly overwhelmed me.

Love Online

While the other couples told their stories, Gina Gould sat on the front row with her husband, Tom, whom she had met as a result of being matched by eHarmony. Gina was crying, and she was not alone. Many people in the studio audience had tears in their eyes, including me.

The host noticed the woman's tears and went to her with the microphone. "Gina, I have been watching you, and all the time these other folks have been talking, you have been crying. I want you to tell me why."

"I am very touched by their stories," Gina said, "because it reminds me of our story, too. I had been widowed for three years, with four children to care for. I wanted to remarry and there were times that I felt ready, but I wanted it to be the right time for my children. I couldn't just marry anybody. The man had to be my spouse, but he also had to be a father to my children.

"One Friday night I was home by myself, painting my basement, and I was suddenly overcome by an unbelievable loneliness, unlike anything that I had ever experienced before. I just knew that I didn't want to be alone anymore. The very next Saturday I was listening to the radio—I had never listened to that station before; I don't even know how it happened to be tuned in to that spot on my dial. I wasn't even listening closely because I was driving, going to pick up my kids, and thinking about something else.

"But then I heard Dr. Warren talking about eHarmony. He said that singles should have a list of 'must haves and can't stands.' That caught my ear because I already had a list of things I wanted and things I knew I couldn't tolerate in a relationship. I went online the following Tuesday, and Tom was one of my first two matches."

Tom had been divorced after eighteen years of marriage. "I felt that I might be single for the rest of my life," said Tom. "I didn't know whether I even wanted to go through the whole dating process again; just the hassles of doing that were depressing. I have four children, just as Gina. There were so many activities with my kids that I didn't have time to really think about what I was going to do with the rest of my life, as far as finding a new potential mate for me.

"In April I heard about eHarmony and realized that I had actually bought some of Dr. Warren's books before that. In one book, he mentioned the ten 'must haves and can't stands.' That intrigued me and I thought, *Well, I'll give it a try.* I didn't really have any expectations. I logged on and filled out the questionnaire and received my personal profile. I was very impressed how accurate the profile was. That gave me more encouragement. I waited about two or three weeks and finally got a match. It was Gina.

"We started to communicate within eHarmony's site, following their suggestions. The more we went through each stage, the more I was impressed. I thought, *Wow, this is really amazing!* The more we talked, the more I realized that we were on the same page about everything—politically, spiritually, and so many other areas that I thought were important. Finally, we went to open communications and we started e-mailing each other. Eventually, we exchanged phone numbers, and finally we started talking on the phone—for hours!

"We actually dated six months before we got married."

Gina offered a keen insight: "Compatibility, of course, is the key in the matching process, but it is just the beginning. It follows through right into the marriage relationship. The joy in having that compatibility is just phenomenal. We are not spending a lot of energy just trying to get along, so we are much more free to enjoy our lives."

SOME OF THE STORIES the couples shared on the radio show that day were heart-gripping. For instance, Louise and Todd Kuyper had both been bereft of their partners after many years of marriage. Louise told her story through her tears. "My husband passed away on Thanksgiving Day," she said. "We'd been married for thirty-five years.

"I had a lot of good friends, and my family is a loving family, but that didn't take the place of my marriage partner.

"About a year after my husband died, a friend gave me an article written by Dr. Warren about his dad being elderly and lonely, and eventually remarrying. The eHarmony address was on the bottom of it. My friend's daughter talked her mom and me into going to the library to go online, because I didn't even own a computer. Her daughter helped us to go through the material on the Web site.

"My son encouraged me, too. 'Mom, you are too young to be alone,' he said. 'You need to meet someone.'

"I said, 'There isn't anybody my age that I would consider.' I was crying all the time."

Todd, too, was unfamiliar with computers. A retired high school art teacher, working with computers had not been required of him during his tenure. But besides their computer illiteracy, Todd and Louise also shared a common pain. Said Todd, "I had been married for forty-one years, and my wife left me. It was very sad and heartbreaking, and I was very lonely. I heard Dr. Warren on the radio, and since I didn't know how to work a computer, I talked to a friend who used a computer in his business. He taught me how to get online and take the profile.

"It took three months for eHarmony to find a match for me. In the meantime, I e-mailed them and asked, 'What's the matter? Is there something wrong with me?' They said, 'No, we are just trying to do what is best for you.' They did, believe you me. Finally, I got five matches all at one time. I eliminated three of them pretty easily. There were two women left that I was interested in, so I struck up a conversation with both of them. One of them was Louise. As it turned out, the other woman honestly confessed to me that she was more interested in somebody else, which made my choice easier. My relationship with Louise blossomed and we got married September first of last year."

DEBORAH AND ROB RUDE'S match was another example of individuals who had few possibilities for marital happiness due to living in a community that did not lend itself to their finding a partner with similar interests. Deborah told us her story first.

"I am from Van Meter, Iowa," she said, "a small town of less than nine hundred people. I was a single parent for eight years. I have four fine sons whom I am homeschooling. Dealing with the effects of an abusive marriage and trying to heal from the wounds, I was involved in therapy and a support group to learn more about myself. I didn't want to repeat the same mistakes that led me into that first marriage.

"I heard about eHarmony in September, shortly after they went online. I had not dated anyone for eight years, but I decided that eHarmony was a safer way for me to get to know someone. So I went on the Web site, and it took me over three hours to fill out those forms! But I was amazed how accurate the profile was. It was right on.

"I probably wouldn't have taken a chance on the Internet at large. Especially because I was busy raising four sons of my own, working three jobs, and homeschooling my boys; there wasn't any time. In all my relationships through church and all my boys' sports activities, I was very guarded. I had been wounded and hurt, and I was very fearful.

"Over the next few months, I received a half dozen or more matches that I explored. I learned a lot about myself, and learned a lot about my fears and my hopes.

"It wasn't until December that I heard from a guy in Las Vegas. When I got this profile and it said from Las Vegas, Nevada, I just threw my head back and laughed. I said, 'Right, like anything *good* could come from Vegas!' So I just set it aside."

Rob filled us in on what was going on in his life about that same time. He admitted, "I am one of those statistics Dr. Warren speaks about that married the wrong person the first time around. After fourteen years of trying to mix oil and water, my first wife decided that was enough; she wanted out.

"I had been really involved with my work, and I really wasn't looking for a mate. In fact, I had just resigned myself that there was nobody in Las Vegas with whom I wanted to connect. I was going to die old and lonely like my dad had done. It was a depressing thought, but it was a reality.

"One day I turned on the radio for some background noise as I was cleaning my house, and I heard the interview with this guy about some Internet dating service. My first thought was, *You've got to be kidding; they normally interview some pretty credible people on that show.* So I switched the channel. There were two other radio stations in the area that I usually listened to, but for some reason, they were both filled with static that day. I turned back to the Internet guy; I heard the Web site announced, but I really didn't pay a lot of attention to it. Later that night, I couldn't sleep, so I got out of bed and went to my computer. I logged on to eHarmony and don't even remembering filling out the profile. An hour and a half later, I completed it, punched in my credit-card number, pressed the 'Send' button, and up pops Deb! She was my first match. But when I saw she was from Iowa, I turned off my computer and went to bed!

"I received a few more matches subsequent to that, but nobody that I wanted to pursue. About a week or two later, I reconsidered Deb, and I knew right away after the first few communications with her that this was the lady I wanted to get to know better. We dated for eight months before we got married."

Deborah offered hope to other singles listening to their story on the radio. "I just want to encourage those people who feel that they have been forgotten, and they feel they're without hope," she said. "There is hope. There is somebody out there that can treat your pain like gold and can cherish your heart, wounds and all. Someone with whom you can share a lifelong love."

HAD WE SPENT MILLIONS of dollars on radio commercials, we could never have achieved the same response as the interviews on that nationally syndicated radio show elicited. That truly was a pivotal point for eHarmony, and we've never had time to think about closing the doors since then.

As we ended the broadcast that day, I told the host, "We hope that these ten couples we've heard here today, who represent two hundred couples that have gotten married as a result of being matched on eHarmony, will turn into five thousand couples. If we dare to dream a big dream, way down the line, I hope that one by one we can reduce the divorce rate one percentage point at a time. Every time that we reduce the divorce rate by one percentage point, it will affect one million people in a generation."

Today, we know there have been far more than six thousand marriages that began by meeting on eHarmony. Certainly, not every person who tries eHarmony enjoys these satisfying results. But we will never stop working to make it possible for every person in the world who wants to find their soul mate to find him or her. I deeply believe there is a soul mate for every person who is emotionally healthy. And I am committed to helping them find each other.

Allow me to show you what I mean.

CHAPTER 2

Finding Your Soul Mate

I'VE SPENT NEARLY my entire life trying to help people develop better relationships. I've been particularly passionate about trying to improve the state of marriages, finding keys that will unlock the doors to marital bliss for everyone I meet.

When we began eHarmony, we didn't want to be merely another "Internet dating service," many of which had all sorts of stigmas and negative connotations attached to them. We intended right from the beginning to be a "relationship-building resource." In fact, we made it quite clear: "If you're not seriously looking for a long-term involvement, don't waste your time or money on eHarmony." Our stated goal was to not simply provide people with matches, introducing them and putting them in touch with each other inside a "safe" environment; we wanted to match two people in the best possible relationship that would culminate in a happy and fulfilled marriage for a lifetime.

Early on, we were advised by friends and competitors alike to avoid the "M" word. "Nobody wants to talk about marriage," they said. A top CEO from one of the largest online dating services in the world gave me a friendly warning before we launched our Web site. "I would advise you, don't talk about the M-word (marriage)," he said, "because that will push singles away." Moreover, he also told us, "Nobody is going to take a 430-some-item questionnaire. If your questionnaire takes more than twenty minutes to complete," he said, "you are doomed to fail. People simply won't take the time to finish it."

He was essentially saying: "We don't think the majority of people out there are serious enough about finding a marriage partner that they will take the time to think carefully through the questionnaire and do what you are asking them to do."

I disagreed. I said, "I don't believe that. Almost all singles would like to be married—if they could be married well, if they could be matched with and be married happily to the person with whom they have the broadest base of compatibility."

Rather than avoiding the "M-word," I instructed our eHarmony staff, "Talk about marriage. Talk about how to have a great marriage. Talk about finding your soul mate for life. That is what people fundamentally want."

Soul mate? What's a soul mate?

When I first began using the term, some groups worried that I had morphed from a respected psychologist into a new age guru of some sort. But after thousands of hours of research, we discovered that "soul mate" was not only a universal term to which everyone can relate, but that everyone is looking for a soul mate when considering a person for a long-term match.

"Soul mate" is not a spooky term shrouded in mystery or a concept that we need to be wary of because of some perceived cultish connection or weird religious connotations. At eHarmony when we speak of soul mates, we are talking about two people who enjoy broad-based compatibility; they fit together.

A soul mate is to his or her soul mate as a Mercedes Benz automobile door is to the Mercedes auto frame. They fit together perfectly; they match. You wouldn't want to put a Chrysler door on a Mercedes car; you wouldn't even want to put a Cadillac, Lexus, or a BMW door on the Mercedes body. Although each one may be a marvelous door in its own right, it would not be the perfect match for the Mercedes automobile.

Similarly, there are many men and women "out there" who might be compatible, who might offer some measure of safety or security, who may be able to shield each other from the heat or the cold to some degree, or keep the rain from falling on one another, but they are not ideal matches for each other. When you find the person with whom you can have the most genuine harmony on the twenty-nine dimensions of a good relationship, you have found your soul mate.

For instance, Linda and Ben have similar intelligence levels. That is one important operational aspect of being soul mates. They also match well in their work ethics, both having grown up in rural north-eastern industrial towns. They are both extremely affectionate, which would lead, they could assume, to a similar level of sexual passion; they are both high-energy people, extremely goal-oriented and ambitious. They love to exercise together, but they are equally comfortable basking in the sun on a white-sand beach. Their list of similarities is long and full, and they match well in many of the essential twenty-nine dimensions. Equally important, they have no major problems such as character disorders or depression. In only a few areas are they dissimilar. For instance, Linda loves working with numbers, while Ben is more of an artist.

Ben and Linda also have spiritual orientations that overlap; they are compatible when it comes to their belief in God and their understanding about how he works in the world and in their lives. The spiritual dimension of a good relationship is an area that is often overlooked, to the couple's eventual displeasure. In an interview with well-known Los Angeles talk show host Dennis Prager, I mentioned that spiritual compatibility is one of the important elements in a good relationship, and it is one of the most difficult to analyze. Just because two people are both "spiritual" does not mean they match. Their spiritual understanding and desires may be worlds apart. On the other hand, after matching thousands of men and women, I've seen extremely few soul mates who were not matched in the spiritual dimension.

All in all, Linda and Ben enjoy a broad-based compatibility. If their personal chemistry matches and they continue to pursue the relationship, I would not be surprised to find them enjoying a happy marriage together for years to come. That is my sincere desire for every person who wants to be well matched and married.

Is a Picture Worth a Thousand Words?

When we first began eHarmony, we encouraged people to take their time in placing pictures on the site. We later changed our policy and

allowed singles to post their pictures at any point they felt ready . . .
and safe. Naturally, many were more than willing to put up their
photos the moment they signed on to the site. Even with the photos
available, we continued to encourage people to fall in love from the
inside out. We didn't want to match people based on their appearances
or their bank accounts. We wanted to match them on their characters,
values, and other dimensions. Unfortunately, we soon discovered that
men especially balked at pursuing a relationship before they were
pleased with a woman's appearance.

Recently, a man in his early thirties looked at me and did a double
take. "Aren't you Dr. Neil Clark Warren?"

"Yes, I am," I answered.

"Great to meet you," he said. "I'm a member on eHarmony."

"Wonderful!" I said. "How's it going?"

"Not so good," he replied with a downcast expression.

"Why? Not enough matches?"

"No, I have plenty of matches," he answered, "but I'm not going
to get involved with anyone until I can see their picture!"

The young man's response was typical of many males on our site.
Many men are focused on the appearance of the young women, and
they are reluctant to pursue a relationship based on inner qualities.
Those who do, however, inevitably find that their relationship is significantly better when it doesn't depend so much on the external
qualities.

Certainly, appearance is important and, in most cases, you should
not marry someone to whom you are not physically attracted, but the
physical aspect is only one part of a good relationship.

Our idea is that it is easier to make a determination about the
external appearance of a person after you have gotten to know the
internal person, rather than trying to get to know the internal person
after you have already prejudiced your decision based on his or her
external appearance.

Besides, in your quest for your soul mate, it is far more important
to discover who you are as a person, what you want from life, and
what values you want to live with. Then, when your soul mate comes
along, you'll be ready to meet that special person.

*   *   *

AT eHARMONY, we believe that all twenty-nine components must be considered in a good relationship. Realistically, we cannot always find a perfect match in all dimensions for every person, but clearly that is the goal. Sadly, many people never even consider more than a few essential factors. If you were to ask ten people on the street or at the shopping mall, "What qualities do you consider most important in a good marriage?" most of them would begin hemming and hawing after about five or six common characteristics. "It's important to be nice. You have to be willing to communicate. Good sex. A sense of humor is a must . . . er, ah . . ." and the list gets short from there.

For years, even trained counselors have relied on a relatively short list of compatibility issues. When I broach the subject to these professionals, I'm often amazed at the incredulous answers I receive. "Tell me; what are the most important dimensions on which people need to be matched when making a lifetime choice in a marriage partner?"

"Well, money, sex, and communication are the three biggest issues most couples struggle with. Get those right and you will probably have a pretty good marriage."

As a matter of fact, if you were to ask the dimension question to most community leaders or marriage counselors, surprisingly few of them could provide more than ten of the twenty-nine crucial variables to consider.

Historically, religious groups have always considered spiritual compatibility as paramount, and rightfully so. More recently, they have become much more straightforward in talking about chemistry, emphasizing the value of a strong, healthy physical attraction between marriage partners.

Sometimes, religious organizations place a surprising amount of emphasis on appearance, especially a "clean-cut, wholesome" appearance. They also promote the concept of hard work, and teach a set of values that espouses helping the underdog, saving money, and giving a percentage of one's income to charity. On the other hand, some religious leaders have encouraged people to get married simply on the basis of spiritual similarities or, frankly, as a legitimate means of reducing sexual temptation. While these areas may indeed be major issues for many singles, if two people are not well matched in the remainder of the twenty-nine dimensions, the couple will soon experience difficulties in their relationship.

The world at large is even more wishy-washy about mutual compatibility; the culture is satisfied with an extremely thin, narrow base of compatibility, usually settling for five main qualities:

1. *Appearance.* Everybody wants somebody who looks good according to the accepted, contemporary standards of attractiveness.
2. *Chemistry.* You must be physically attracted to the person.
3. *A sense of humor.* We all want someone who not only makes us smile, but can laugh a lot and enjoy life.
4. *Status.* Most singles prefer somebody with a level of social status slightly higher than their own.
5. *A front-end personality.* A person with the ability to make you feel comfortable in talking with them.

Most of the popular television programs and movies nowadays would imply that if you can find someone with these five characteristics, that's enough on which to base a solid marriage relationship. Because the influence of television is so pervasive in our society, many younger partners especially are deceived into settling for thinly based compatibility.

The typical high school senior has watched twelve thousand hours of television. He or she has been in the classroom eight thousand hours, so television teaches more than the classroom does. And TV suggests that this thinly based compatibility is all modern couples need to have a good relationship. Unquestionably, one of the main reasons so many marriages are rapidly failing today is because we have let television convince us that a narrowly based compatibility is sufficient.

But wait a minute!

What about character? Does the person tell the truth? Does she cheat on her taxes? If he lies to other people, he will eventually lie to you. And if he or she will lie or cheat a little, inevitably they will lie or cheat a lot.

What about emotional health? Does the person sometimes slide into deep troughs of depression? Does he or she display manic behavior or addictions? Drugs, sex, alcohol, gambling, eating disorders, or other addictions can destroy the best of relationships. Any type of addiction will drain a marriage of joy, energy, and vitality, and if not corrected, possibly even of life itself. Please understand! *No marriage can ever be stronger than the emotional health of the least healthy partner.*

How does the person you are considering as a potential marriage partner deal with anger? Does he have his temper under control? Anger mismanagement causes more divorces, I believe, than any other single factor. Many people simply cannot handle their anger, and they take it out on their spouses. Sadly, husbands often take out their anger on their wives, and wives often take out their anger on the children, thus perpetuating a downward spiral into the next generation. Anger, of course, is often the means a person uses to attempt to handle his or her pain. But it can destroy an otherwise good relationship if it is not expressed correctly.

THE HEART OF THIS BOOK is to help you explore the twenty-nine dimensions of a good relationship, providing you with some practical criteria to keep in mind as you evaluate the next person with whom you go out or consider for a potential relationship.

"Oh, I'll just know inside," one thirty-four-year-old man said when I asked him what standard he used in evaluating potential marriage partners. "My dad always told me that I'd just know it deep down in my gut when the right woman for me comes along."

Isn't that ironic? That fellow's father probably spent more time teaching him how to tie his shoelaces than he spent teaching his son how to make the most important decision in his life.

And that's what the choice of a marriage partner is!

The most important emotional choice that any man or woman ever makes is the decision about the person they intend to marry. On the human level, no other decision we make is fraught with such powerful emotions and long-term ramifications. With whom are you going to live, eat thousands of meals, have children, go on vacation, make your financial plans, and pursue your important dreams and goals in life? Clearly, the person who will occupy that position in your life should not be selected lightly.

Yet many people do. "Oh, I'll just know when the right person comes along." Really? How will you know? On what basis will you make that decision? By what criteria will you sort out the possibilities?

Some people say, "I don't want to have to think that hard about finding my mate. I just want to fall in love! I want it to happen naturally." These people have obviously watched too many movies. They believe in the myth of fairy-tale meetings and magical marriages such as those experienced by Cinderella, Snow White, and other story characters. Their theme song is "Some Enchanted Evening"; across a crowded room, you will see a stranger, and your life will be forever changed. Does that happen occasionally? Of course it does! And perhaps that is why we make such a big deal about it—because it is so unusual rather than the norm.

Some people have been hurt so badly in previous relationships that they have given up hope of ever experiencing true love. But even those people who are reluctant to say so publicly have a deep desire within to be partnered with someone who will love them for who they are, and to love someone for the rest of their lives. And I want you to fall in love, too. But I want you to fall in love for all the right reasons.

I ONCE CONDUCTED a study that examined one hundred couples who enjoyed "highly successful marriages." I inevitably discovered that they were well matched on the same twenty-nine dimensions, including intellect, ambition, energy level, and others. The more the couple matched, the greater their satisfaction level with their marriage.

Consider a woman who is forty years old. Of all the men in the world, there are no doubt at least a thousand with whom she would match ten or more of the twenty-nine dimensions; perhaps she would match with hundreds of men in twenty or more of the dimensions. Possibly, she'd match with scores of fellows in twenty-six to twenty-eight dimensions. But our goal is to find her as many men as possible who match her in as many of the twenty-nine dimensions as possible.

Be careful though! Just because a person matches you does not necessarily mean that he or she is your soul mate. You may have many matches before you actually discover your soul mate. But you must start with that broad-based compatibility and then work to develop closeness and intimacy.

John, a fine fellow in his forties, had never been married, and he received more than 480 matches on eHarmony. That's nearly five hundred women that our highly accurate, computer matching system determined were compatible with this man, based on their deeper values and what they wanted out of life. But on receiving each match, after he'd carefully considered it, he'd say, "No. She's not the right one." He knew himself well, and he knew what he was looking for, and he refused to compromise or lower his standards. He believed it was only a matter of time and perseverance before he was matched with his soul mate. And he was right!

Finally, he was matched with Cyndi, a woman from McKinney, Texas, not far from where he lived. John later said that he knew immediately from their written communications that Cyndi was a good match for him. They moved from e-mails to open communication to dating. "Think of it," he said, "I've been searching for this person for forty-two years, and now I've found her!"

Could he have been happy with any of the other 479 matches? Probably so. But it is unlikely that any of these other women would have been his soul mate. The woman with whom he shares the broadest base of compatibility is his soul mate, and he knew her when he found her.

He said, "The first time I talked with her, I knew that she was the one. We were perfect for each other!"

Sometimes the person who is your soul mate may be a "diamond in the rough." He or she may not look like your dream mate at first blush; he or she may not satisfy all the images about which you have fantasized in your mind. But if you are well matched on the twenty-nine dimensions, it would be worth your time to at least consider that person and give him or her a chance. If nothing else, you will have formed a friendship with a person who is a lot like you.

I was convinced from the beginning of my career that despite the so-called "liberated ladies," "swinging singles scenes," and the overblown benefits of bachelor pads, many singles were lonely and genuinely wanted to find somebody to love. More than that, most wanted to find the "love of their life."

For many singles, the primary reason for their lack of success was because their circle of friendships and opportunities was far too small. Perhaps they hailed from a small, rural community, or the number of available men and women in their community circles was extremely limited. But what if they had more people from which to choose? Not two or three possible mates from which to select, but two or three thousand! I became convinced that the chances of their finding a soul mate could be increased exponentially.

Don't be deceived by the modern-day emphasis on quick-fix relationships. Meet someone, spend a brief amount of time getting to know them, and the next thing you know, you're walking down the aisle at your wedding. That is a dangerous myth foisted on the public and perpetuated by many movies and much of the music and media of our day.

In the late 1960s and early 1970s, relationship-based television programs such as *The Dating Game* and *The Newlywed Game* proved to be popular. In more recent years, television has once again become enamored with matching men and women romantically, cranking out new "reality shows" almost faster than the local TV listings can keep up with them. Unfortunately, many of these programs set relationship building back immeasurably, giving the impression that a potentially good marriage partner can be determined on the basis of appearance, money, sexual "energy," or other first impressions. All of this is done with cameras and microphones hovering everywhere the couple go, and culminates within a thirteen-week series or less.

These shows make me sad. The emphasis on superficial qualities not only will lead the participants to poor relationships, but viewers by the millions will be influenced by the misguided images and mistaken messages.

Be smart; take all the time you need to make a wise decision about your marriage partner. Remember, a bad marriage is a thousand

times worse than no marriage at all. Better to be single th
married to the wrong person. Don't settle for second best; .
nothing less than the love of your life—your soul mate.

How will you know that person? Let's take a closer look at how .
twenty-nine dimensions that must be considered can help you in
finding your soul mate.

Is There Hope for Me?

One of the most vivacious people to appear in our eHarmony television advertisements over the years is a young woman named Alison
Strobel. A lively, bright, extremely attractive young woman, Alison is
the only daughter of Lee Strobel, one of America's most highly respected and best-selling authors.

Alison received one hundred matches on eHarmony. She analyzed each match carefully and none seemed quite right for her. But
when she was matched with Daniel Morrow, she knew she had found
her soul mate. Ironically, Alison was Daniel's very first match! But he
knew that she was the woman for him.

At their wedding, Lee Strobel stood up and said of his daughter
and her husband, "Alison and Daniel are the two best-matched
people I've ever known."

And they really are!

We've probably aired more commercials featuring Alison and
Daniel than any other couple. They are just so happy!

In one spot, Alison radiantly exudes, "I love my husband!" and
the viewers instinctively can tell that this marriage is going to last,
just by seeing the truth shining through Alison's countenance. While
we can't guarantee that every person on eHarmony will find the same
joy and satisfaction Alison and Daniel have discovered, that is our
goal. We know the system works; we know that matching in the
twenty-nine dimensions of a good relationship can help you find
people from around the world, or around the block, with whom you
are highly compatible across a broad spectrum.

But what does compatibility really mean, and where can you
find it?

...tionizing how you see potential marriage part-
...nt, how you see yourself. If you will follow
... out for you, I can guarantee that you will
...hieve the relationship of your dreams, and
...ee that you will greatly improve the likelihood of
...ve of your life.

...s a pretty astounding claim, isn't it? Yes, it is, and at this point
in my life, I'd have no reason to pump up your hopes if I didn't honestly believe in the realistic possibility of discovering your soul mate.

During the nearly four decades that I was a practicing clinical psychologist in Pasadena, I personally counseled more than seven thousand people about their painful relationships. Much of that pain had
to do with either getting involved in a difficult, unhappy marital situation, or not being able to find true love.

I thought, *I would love to do something for single people around the
world to give each individual the best possible chance of finding the love of
his or her life.* Not only do I want you to find love, I want you to find a
love so true that you and your partner have no doubt about your potential for long-term happiness.

As I mentioned previously, I'm convinced that the selection of a
marriage partner is the most important, far-reaching decision you
will ever make. Let me tell you why. For the rest of your life, every day,
you will wake up with this person; much of your day will revolve
around this person in one way or another, whether you are at work or
at home. You will come home to this person, eat dinner with this person, sit and talk with this person and, hopefully, you will go to bed
with this person. When you wake up in the morning, this person will
still be there! You will have a lot of thoughts about this person all day
long, because this person and you will have numerous things in common, including your children, your money, your plans about your
careers, and plans about your retirement. Think about that. One person . . . for the rest of your life! That's a lot of togetherness! Yet that's
what marriage is supposed to be, and that's what marriage can be, if
you select the correct partner. It is such an important decision that it
should be made with great clarity and with as much wisdom, insight,
and expertise as you can muster.

If you do this well, you will set yourself up for the greatest experience you will ever have on earth—a relationship in which you have one person who loves you unconditionally; a person who knows you at your best and at your worst, and still loves you! You will have a person you can deeply trust and someone you genuinely like and with whom you want to spend the majority of your time; one person who can validate you consistently, and for whom you can also consistently provide personal validation. If you make the right choice, you will have more enjoyment and enrichment in your life than you ever dreamed possible!

Unfortunately, our culture hasn't given due respect to this decision. It hasn't given finding the love of your life and finding your soul mate the rightful position of preeminence and careful analysis that the ramifications of marriage merit. Keep in mind those staggering statistics mentioned previously—of all first marriages in the United States, 20 percent of them are history within five years. Thirty-three percent end within ten years. Forty-three percent are over within fifteen years. And we know the current divorce rate skyrockets to at least 50 percent. In addition, about 6 percent of all first marriages end in separation, but the two people don't get a divorce because they don't plan to get married again. Moreover, of the approximately 50 percent of those first marriages that stay together, if you talk to the husbands and wives and question them carefully, you will quickly discover that in half of those marriages, one or both participants will say, "I am not happy."

I don't wish this to be discouraging, but merely a strong dose of reality. If you don't do a good job of matching yourself with someone else, you are basically rolling the dice and relying on luck. And like the gambling tables in Las Vegas casinos, when you leave to chance such a serious relationship as marriage, luck will most often be against you. The odds are at least 50 percent or better that you will experience a devastating divorce (there is no such thing as an "amicable" divorce; all divorces are disastrous, and those involving children always leave severe scars on the innocents). Beyond that, you run an additional 25 percent possibility that you will be miserable in a marriage. Mark it well: Only 25 percent of marriages survive happily. "And they lived happily ever after" for many people is a colossal hoax!

But there is also good news! (Whew! Aren't you glad of that?)

After countless hours of meticulous, empirical research, a team of psychologists and I have discovered the twenty-nine dimensions that happily married people have taken seriously, and unhappily married people have matched poorly. Simply put, if you learn to recognize these twenty-nine dimensions and discover how to determine whether you are well matched with a particular person, you will have a nearly foolproof litmus test to determine your potential for enjoying a lifetime of great marital success—or not—with that person.

What all is involved? In the pages ahead, we'll examine all twenty-nine of the key components that must be considered in a good marriage, but first let me mention a few highlights. First and foremost is emotional health, because it is foundational to this kind of relationship. Having good emotional health is more important to marriage partners than any other single dimension. More about that later, but for now, let me simply say that you don't want to marry someone who is depressed, or someone who has a character disorder or who just thinks about life much differently than you do.

A second broad principle that we will look at more closely in this book is *similarities*. You may be surprised to learn that the best marriage partner for you is somebody who is a whole lot like you! If you find somebody who has good character and is emotionally healthy, and then you get somebody who is a lot like you, the two of you will have a tremendous chance to make that relationship work.

Years ago, some experts encouraged people searching for their mates to find somebody much different from themselves. The idea made sense. Where I am weak, and my wife is strong, we can balance out our deficits. Moreover, everyone knows that opposites attract. Right?

Yes, opposites often do attract . . . at first . . . while you are dating. But while opposites may attract in dating, in marriage, opposites tend to *attack*! Each other! You'll be much better off in your search for a soul mate if you limit your search to people who are a lot like you.

"Oh, Dr. Warren, I'm too old to find a mate," one woman in her late fifties lamented. "I could never find a match at my age."

"Oh, no; you are never too old to fall in love!" I encouraged her. "Anybody, at any age or stage of life, can find that match, that soul mate, if willing to work at it." I wasn't just trying to placate her or make her feel good. I'm convinced that if a person is persistent and patient enough, if he or she follows the principles in this book, if he is on the lookout, and she is ready for a relationship, they can have the wonderful experience of finding their soul mate.

Barry, a never-married successful businessman in his late forties, found his soul mate by following our principles. He gushed, "It's amazing! This woman is so much a part of me, and is so well matched with me, we feel as though we were meant for each other from the beginning of the world."

Barb, his bride-to-be, put it succinctly: "Barry understands me like nobody else on this planet. He gets me!"

That may not be the most profound definition of compatibility, but it is a good one. He gets me. She gets me. At a deep level, this person understands and cares about who I am and what is important to me.

At eHarmony, we know of numerous thriving relationships between people who, because of their ages, had long since given up hope of finding true love. In early 2004, NBC News covered the wedding of a woman and a gentleman who had met after finding each other at eHarmony.

"What's so unusual about that?" you ask.

The bride was eighty-one years old, and the groom was eighty years of age! And they were as madly in love as two people in their twenties!

My own dad found love in his latter years. Just about a year after my mom passed away, my dad decided to remarry. He and my mom had been married for seventy years, and although they hadn't known the degree of happiness and compatibility that I would have liked for them, they loved each other and our family.

I served as my dad's psychologist for his "premarital counseling" prior to his second marriage. During one of our counseling sessions, Dad said, "Neil, I have to get married again for two reasons."

"Oh, really? What are they, Dad?"

"One, I am so lonely; and two, my sex drive is so strong."

The man was ninety-two years of age!

I didn't know whether to laugh or to shout aloud, "Yes, sir!" For a moment, I thought of pulling out one of the oft-quoted lines from the baggage of my family's extremely conservative religious upbringing, and whispering softly, "Dad, we don't talk about things like that." But of course I didn't. Instead, I was rejoicing that I have Dad's genes!

I come from a family that believes deeply in marriage. As I said, my folks were married for seventy years, and my two sisters have been married to their husbands for more than sixty years. Marylyn and I have been married for more than forty-five years, and Marylyn's and my three daughters are all happily married; the Warren family believes in marriage. For all the jokes and jabs the institution of marriage receives, it's been such a good thing for our family, and we highly recommend it—when you are married to the right person.

When our first daughter, Lorrie, was fourteen years old, I started saying, "I don't want you to rely on luck. I want you to know specifically what it takes to be in the group of very happily married people." I spent a lot of time thinking about it, and I have written several books and numerous articles on the subject. This is not just a professional interest of mine; this is something in which I have a deep personal concern.

I'm convinced that if you get this right, life can be grand; but if you marry the wrong person, it will be the source of more human pain than any other irritant in the world. Just think about two people who link their lives together and have children together, and then discover they've made a tragic mistake. "We aren't well matched." They break up that marriage, and it is like peeling the skin off their souls. Divorce is like trying to separate two pieces of paper that have been glued together. Somebody usually gets ripped apart in the process. It is painful. I have watched many children go through such pain because their parents weren't well matched before the wedding day. I have watched many husbands and wives go through much pain. Believe me, if you make a wrong choice in your marriage partner, it is excruciatingly painful.

Can you live a fulfilled and satisfied life if you remain single all your days? Absolutely. In fact, we will emphasize throughout these pages that the key to satisfaction is to get yourself a big and healthy life. Then if you find the person to whom you want to be married for a lifetime, it will be like putting frosting on a cake. You will have so much more to give your future spouse. If you don't ever find that person, you will still have a big, healthy, good life. More important, you will have made every single day count!

Will This Really Work?

Imagine you are in a room with twenty-five people of the opposite sex, all single, all roughly your age, all potential marriage candidates. You have three minutes to spend with each of these individuals to determine which ones you like the most and in whom you can see potential for a possible long-term relationship. After seventy-five minutes, I'll ask you, "With which of these people would you like to have further contact?"

If you are similar to most people, you will probably have three to five people in mind.

"Okay," I say, "now tell me, of these twenty-five, what was there about each of the individuals you selected that hinted you'd like to have further contact with them?"

"Oh, I like number seven's smile . . . and number fourteen, he just seems like a really nice guy. And number ten, oh, my! Well, I like the way he just opened up to me. I could see it in his eyes; he talked to me, and I just fell in love with him right there."

"She's so gorgeous! Are you kidding? Look at her! What's not to love?"

What do you think your chances of finding your soul mate in that group of people might be? Fifty-fifty? Twenty percent probability? Ten, maybe? Two? *None?*

Okay, now let me take you right across the hall to another room where we have twenty-five attractive persons, all single, all your age, and I am going to give you three minutes to be with each of those twenty-five people. But these are twenty-five individuals who have been carefully selected to participate in this experiment because they have all proved to be compatible with you in all or nearly all of the twenty-nine key dimensions that must be examined in a good relationship. These are twenty-five people who have the qualities that we know will be a good match with you.

"Spend three minutes with each one, and then tell me with whom you would like to spend further time."

Would your confidence level rise? Absolutely! Why? Because you already know that thanks to our prescreening of these individuals, these are your kind of people. With this bunch, you can't miss! You know going into that room we have already matched you in intelligence, energy, curiosity, and all the other important dimensions of a good relationship. If you walk in and detect mutual chemistry with any one of these people, you are going to be in great shape!

That is basically what we do at eHarmony every day for singles from around the world, and that's why we know the plan works!

Can you still fall in love at first sight? Sure, and that relationship will work, as long as the person with whom you are falling in love is a good match and has all the other important characteristics.

Unfortunately, if you are attracted to someone at first sight who is not a good match in the twenty-nine dimensions, chances are high that the relationship will last for about six to eight months after you get married. Then the excitement will evaporate. You will be like an airplane, flying at thirty thousand feet for a while, but then you will suddenly run out of fuel. Unless you have broad-based compatibility, you will cruise along until suddenly your relationship takes a nosedive.

In contrast, I'm convinced that the weddings of people who have been matched by eHarmony will go the distance. When two people match in the twenty-nine variables we know to be crucial, they can be sure they have "broad-based compatibility." Broad-based compatibility is what it takes for two people to walk together down the road of life and to make it through the difficult times as well as the good times. Understand, having broad-based compatibility does not mean you must be perfectly matched in every issue of life; that is an impossibility. But true soul mates are well enough matched over a wide spectrum that they can make it no matter what life throws at them.

While eHarmony is a high-tech means of matching you with individuals on the basis of the twenty-nine dimensions, you do not have to sign up with our matching and relationship-building program or any other to benefit from these twenty-nine principles. Clearly, the task of finding a person with whom you have broad-based compatibility is a complex challenge. You may discover that on your own you are not able to assess your position on each of these scales, while simultaneously assessing another person's position. If you are like me, you may conclude that the task of discovering your soul mate involves too many variables, and you need assistance. But just as you can make a much more intelligent decision about how you want to handle your finances when you know how compounding interest rates can work for or against you, it is possible to make a better choice of a spouse when you understand compatibility and what it takes to make a good marriage—not in theory, but in actual practice!

I sincerely hope that schools, churches, and other civic groups will begin teaching these twenty-nine principles to young people *before* they get involved in relationships. I'm convinced that if we can better educate people about what it takes to maintain a solid marriage, we will be doing both them and our society a great service.

The strongest passion in my heart is that these twenty-nine principles will be helpful to you whether or not you choose to use the resources of eHarmony. Certainly, many people have found eHarmony to be a valuable aid in matching with people of similar values, tastes, and lifestyles. Some people may prefer another of the more than three thousand online matching services (although I can't imagine why!). Other people may simply take the information within these pages and handle matters for themselves.

Regardless of how you decide to go about finding and choosing a mate, you will need to know these principles, and you must get them right.

MOST OF US tend to be rather possessive about our social lives. "I don't know much about art, but I know what I like," some people say as they peruse an art gallery. That's similar to the attitude most of us have when it comes to determining our own destinies in the realm of dating, falling in love, and selecting a marriage partner. "I know what I like," said one thirty-nine-year-old man, "so why would I turn a decision as important as finding a mate over to an online service?"

Perhaps for the same reason you might use an online service to find the best hotel room or airfare—somebody else has done the research for you, so you benefit from more selection, faster results, and usually less cost.

Marylyn and I have traveled around the country interviewing people who have been matched according to our twenty-nine dimensions, and there is no greater thrill for us than to see the expressions of love, joy, and commitment on the faces of these happy couples. When well-matched people find each other, they are pulled to one another like a powerful electromagnet. They feel so strongly; they love so passionately. They are the first to say, "You *can* find the love of your life, and when you do, it will change everything about your focus."

Please understand, you don't have to leave your marital status to fate. You can learn very specific things that will help you; every time you take advantage of one of these ideas, it will better your odds of finding your soul mate. But have no illusions; it takes work. Finding your soul mate probably won't happen by accident. Most likely, your soul mate will not show up on your front porch, ring your doorbell, and say, "I'm here out of the blue, and I came to tell you that we should get married!" It doesn't happen that way. If you are to find your soul mate, it will be because you take the initiative and engage in intentional, positive actions.

I want you to realize that this is not simply psychological guessing. We don't sit in the eHarmony offices, saying, "We have a real good theory here, and we think this will work." No, we *know* that matching in these twenty-nine dimensions works. Careful research utilizing well-developed assessment techniques demonstrates that couples who are carefully matched have significantly stronger relationships. Granted, even the best matching program doesn't work for everybody. You must be emotionally healthy, and you must be emotionally ready for a long-term relationship with someone of the opposite sex. That's why we emphasize so strongly, "Get your life to the place where it is deeply meaningful, regardless of whether you are hoping to meet your soul mate and get married." If you have a meaningful, "big" life, as I like to call it, and you meet somebody that is simply wonderful, your relationship will be that much better because you are bringing more to the table. If you don't meet your soul mate, you will still have a big life, a life filled with joy, significance, and meaning.

TALKING WITH SINGLE ADULTS about their hopes of getting married (or remarried), I often find more skepticism than hope. Many single people are discouraged and disillusioned about the whole process of dating as an adult. They may have dated two or three times and it hasn't worked. The myth of the "swinging single" is just that—a myth! The truth is, over 50 percent of all singles in America have not had a date in more than two years! Even for many of those who have been dating, in the majority of cases things have not been working out well. You may know exactly what I mean. The entire process of meeting new people who might have interests similar to yours has been awkward and difficult.

But can that change? I believe it can, thanks to modern computer technology and the deep well of scientific research from which you can readily draw wisdom nowadays. As I mentioned previously, I have no need at my age to convince somebody they ought to have hope, if there really is no hope. But I sincerely and deeply believe that there is tremendous hope for you to find the love of your life, if you are willing to do what is necessary. After all, if you are looking for the love of your life, it takes only that one person to strike the perfect match with you.

I was doing a seminar in Nashville, Tennessee, a couple of years ago for an audience made up of mostly PhD-level psychologists. Sitting in the front row was an extremely skeptical woman. She didn't heckle or harass me, but she was doubtful that a matchmaking program based on the twenty-nine dimensions of a good relationship could work, and her caustic questions repeatedly reminded the audience of her cynicism.

Fortunately, sitting on the front row on the other side of the auditorium was a woman named Linda who had introduced herself to me prior to the start of the seminar. She said, "Dr. Warren, I am on eHarmony.com, and I got involved with a man that you introduced me to. You matched me with him, and we are getting married in a month!" She said, "I am so pleased and happy."

Throughout the seminar, when my caustic critic voiced her views, I turned to Linda time after time. "Linda, what was your experience on that?" I'd ask. Linda related her experience, which, in most cases, was quite positive.

The cynic kept right on asking more questions, which I fielded, answered, and then pitched to Linda to describe what her practical experience had been in that area. As the seminar proceeded, I could tell that the cynic was softening, but I never dreamed that after all her caustic questions she would actually get on the eHarmony site. A few weeks later, I received an e-mail message from the critic: "I've gotten on eHarmony, and you will probably be shocked, but I am finding some meaning there."

A few weeks later, I got another message in which she said, "You have matched me with somebody, and he looks like a great person for me."

Three weeks later, she wrote, "I just met that person, and we feel that we might have potential . . ."

A few months later, she wrote to tell me, "We have decided to get married!"

She and the man with whom she was matched got married, and they had a baby about a year and a half after their wedding. Now, every year, they send me pictures of their baby. This was a woman who had lost hope of ever being married; that's why she was so skeptical. Yet, finding her soul mate turned out to be the most exciting adventure of her life.

Finding that person isn't a magical moment in which you lock eyes with someone at a party, and everything in life is terrific from then on. Quite the contrary; finding that person with whom you can have all things in common is the most underappreciated complexity in the human experience.

Consider this: You want a person with whom you can share mutual trust at a deep level, someone in whom you have absolute confidence that when he or she tells you something, they don't exaggerate or lie to you; they don't try to manipulate you in any way. You want to be able to put your money with his or her money, and have it in common. If you want to have children, you and your soul mate will teach similar values to those children. You want to have somebody whose interests overlap yours, or who perhaps is willing to learn a new interest. It is a very complex matter to find that person.

The good news is that you are fortunate to be alive today, because it is now possible for a single person to know what the complex issues are regarding compatibility, and to satisfy them in such a fundamental way that you can have deep confidence that your partner is right for you.

Compatibility used to mean that two people liked the same kind of movies or music but, as you will see as we examine the twenty-nine dimensions, compatibility now means a whole lot more. One of our favorite phrases around eHarmony is "Who knew that science and love could be so compatible?"

What we are really saying, of course, is "Who could have guessed that a person's mind is as critical in love as is his or her heart?"

"But Dr. Warren, I feel like I'm dissecting a frog!" one fellow said as I quizzed him about his relationship with a potential spouse. "Won't all this analysis of what goes into a good relationship take all the magic out of love? Won't it destroy all the sparks and the fireworks?"

Quite the opposite! The idea of bringing knowledge into your love life should not destroy the magic; in fact, it can enhance a good relationship. Certainly, you should have those feelings of exhilaration and passion, or you shouldn't get married. But you should also have something else—let's call it "careful thinking." Let's think clearly about these twenty-nine dimensions so you can minimize the chances that your relationship will be unsatisfying, and maximize your chances that this relationship will be romantic and exciting for as long as you and your partner live. When you think clearly about falling in love, the emotional experience is all the grander, because you know that the type of love you are seeking is based not on fickle, transient qualities, but on truth and values that are important to you.

This is about a relationship that was meant to be. If there is anything that makes romantic feelings take flight and soar, it is the sense that this relationship is going to last forever.

To help better understand the twenty-nine matching variables, I've grouped them into four categories:

1. *Screening Dimensions* (designed to help you avoid troublemakers and to prevent you from becoming romantically involved with a problematic person)
2. *Core Personal Dimensions* (These are characteristics in you and your partner that are relatively difficult to alter.)
3. *Necessary Skills That Can Be Developed*
4. *Crucial Qualities That Can Be Developed* (if you both manage your emotional lives well)

You'll understand the reasons for these categories more clearly as we go along and you see how the dimensions fit together. Let's get started! Your soul mate is waiting!

GROUP 1

The Screening Dimensions

MOST PEOPLE whose marriages get in trouble early on choose to overlook problems that already existed on their wedding day. They were simply terribly naive, or they willingly pulled the blinders over their eyes and pretended the problems weren't there. It always amazes me how quickly those blinders come off after the wedding day, and people cry out in despair, "What did I do?"

That's why the first seven dimensions are called "the screening dimensions." These dimensions are intended to be just what the name implies—screens to prevent the bugs from getting into a relationship, screens to keep bad people out of your life, or screens through which your relationship can be run and analyzed to see if it has any serious weaknesses.

The screening dimensions may sound a bit negative, but they are not meant to be. They are, however, intended to be stringent, so for your own good, please don't try to water them down or sugarcoat your relationship in regard to these crucial areas.

These dimensions are not necessarily meant to match you with a particular person. In fact, if you and the person you are considering have a problem in *any* of these areas, these screens may actually prevent you from moving forward in your relationship at this time. If you find that is the case, please muster the courage to do what is right, and in the best interests of you and your partner, by backing away from that relationship.

Understand, these seven dimensions must be considered *no matter who you marry*. If you marry anyone on earth, ever, you must evaluate these seven dimensions. Moreover, you must have a perfect, positive ledger in these seven areas if you hope to have anything beyond a platonic relationship with the person you are considering. If you fare well in all seven of these dimensions, but your partner does not do well in one or two of them, walk away from that relationship. It won't work! To have a truly great marriage, you must be well matched in all of the screening dimensions.

CHAPTER 3

DIMENSION **1** | Good Character

THE FIRST SCREENING dimension you must consider in a potential relationship is *good character*. Don't kid yourself; character matters! And it matters a lot. No marriage will ever thrive if one of the partners has bad character. By character, I mean integrity, honesty, and moral uprightness. Some people refuse to recognize that good character is important. "Oh, does he lie a little? But he's so cute, I don't think that will be a problem."

I can almost guarantee you that it will be!

If one of the partners in a relationship lies, cheats, or steals, that bad character will eventually undermine the relationship. Maybe not at first, but I guarantee you, if the foundation of your relationship is not built on good, strong character, it is only a matter of time until the entire house of cards crumbles.

If you or your partner lies, for instance, the first thing to go in your relationship will be the trust. Brian told his wife, Natalie, that he was going over to Bob's house to play pool with the boys after work. It was his one night out with the guys each week, so Natalie didn't mind. In fact, Brian's being out of the house gave her a chance to catch up on some reading she had wanted to do.

Around 9:30 p.m., Natalie remembered that Brian had received an important phone call from his boss earlier that evening. She dialed Bob's phone number to pass along the message to Brian. Bob's wife, Judy, answered the phone.

"Brian? No, Natalie. Brian hasn't been here all night. Bob is here, though, if you'd like to speak with him."

"Do you mean they are not playing pool?" Natalie asked innocently.

"No, Bob and I are here all by ourselves," Judy replied.

"Isn't this their regular pool game?" Natalie asked.

"Oh, my, no. They haven't had a pool night here for ages," Judy responded.

Natalie was waiting up when Brian crept into the bedroom late that night. "How was the pool game?" she asked.

"Oh, great," Brian replied, surprised that Natalie was still awake.

"Did you win?"

"Oh, no, I played pretty crummy."

"How did Bob do?"

"Oh, Bob did really well. He ran the table several times."

"I'll bet he did."

"Wha—?"

"Brian, where have you been? You smell like smoke, and I talked with Judy earlier tonight, and she said you hadn't been there at all. In fact, you haven't been there any of these past weeks when you've told me that you were going to play pool."

"I can't believe you've been checking up on me!" Brian railed. "So what? So I wasn't playing pool. What's the difference? I was still out with the guys."

"Where, Brian? Where were you?"

"Down at Joe's Bar." Recognizing that he'd been caught, Brian shifted to a different tack. "It really hurts me, Natalie, that you don't trust me . . ." He apologized to her and said that he had just not wanted to worry her.

BY THE TIME Brian came clean to Natalie about his weekly activities, he admitted that he had been playing poker every week and hadn't wanted Natalie to know. Pool or poker, the game was irrelevant to Natalie. What mattered to her, and what Brian failed to understand, was that he had indeed broken their trust.

Trust is an amazing virtue; it will see you through almost any storm, but it is one of the most fragile elements in a relationship.

Once it is broken, regardless of how insignificantly, it takes a long time to repair the breach.

Watch out especially for individuals who have a tendency to tell "convenient truth," enough truth to keep their consciences from bothering them at night, but not enough to be forthright. "Tell him I just stepped out of the office," Chuck instructed his secretary to tell a client whose call he didn't want to take. Chuck then stepped out of the office to get a cup of coffee. Would you trust Chuck? You shouldn't.

Some people get so used to lying that they don't even realize they are doing it anymore. They can look you right in the eyes and lie to you because, in their minds, what they are saying has a kernel of truth to it; therefore, their entire statement is blanketed by truth.

Rick laughed uproariously when Nancy, the woman he was dating, told him about the outlandish tax deductions she had taken, yet she'd never been audited by the Internal Revenue Service. "I can't believe you get away with that!" he marveled.

Rick and Nancy eventually married, and Nancy continued to handle their finances. Imagine Rick's dismay when a few years into their marriage, they were hit with a six-figure bill for Nancy's back taxes.

How can you spot someone with a character disorder? It's not always as easy as it might seem. But watch out for signs that reveal *a diminished sense of conscience*. People who willfully and regularly lie, exaggerate, or cheat have no regard for the rights of others. It's almost as though they feel that they are "above the law"; the rules apply to everybody else but not to them.

Don't be naive. If she lies to someone else, she will eventually lie to you. If he lies a little, eventually he will lie a lot. If she manipulates others to get what she wants, she will attempt to manipulate you as well. If he behaves impulsively toward others, or with no apparent pangs of conscience, he will pay little attention to how his actions impact you, as long as he gets what he wants. Deceit runs deep in his personhood; it is a facet of his personality; his lack of character colors everything he says or does.

You might tend to think that someone with a character disorder looks like the villain in a bad movie—unkempt, foulmouthed, poorly dressed, and abusive in all aspects of his or her behavior. Certainly, that is sometimes the case. But more often, a person with a character disorder has mastered the art of putting on a facade of social acceptability. He or she knows how to gain your confidence and that of other people. The person with a character disorder is often a smooth talker, a charmer, a person who knows how to say just the right thing to get what he or she wants. Often, they can be likable, entertaining, and the life of the party . . . . until you get home. These people are takers rather than givers. If you let a person with a character disorder get close to you, he or she will take everything you have to give, everything they can get, and give you little in return except heartbreak, calamity, and pain.

Just because two people stay together in marriage does not mean they have solved a character disorder. Some people stay together in spite of their partner's despicable character. When that happens, often both partners develop more serious character defects as a result of one partner's propensity to lie, cheat, or steal. Bill had a problem with lying, which eventually led to all sorts of deceit and sexual indiscretions. He had never been totally faithful to Heather before they were married, and it wasn't long after their wedding before he engaged in the first of many extramarital affairs.

Heather suspected that Bill was cheating on her even before the marriage, but she went through with the wedding anyhow. After all, everyone said that they "were the perfect couple," that they looked great together. Heather loved Bill, but her real love was money and prestige. Her goal in life was to be known as the socialite who called the shots. Bill and Heather used one another to get what they wanted, operating warily around each other as one tiger might circle another, looking for an opportunity to gain the advantage. Although Bill and Heather have remained married, their entire relationship is permeated by distrust, suspicion, disdain, and even hatred. It is a sad caricature of what a happy marriage is meant to be.

If there are facets about your potential partner's character that you question—areas such as dishonesty, a tendency to shade the truth or even outright lie, or making light of cheating or stealing—ask yourself a simple question: *Do I really want to spend the rest of my life dealing with these issues?* Because I assure you, if you don't resolve these issues before you are married, they will be exacerbated after the wedding for two main reasons. One, your personal leverage will be less once you are married; and two, his or her motivation to improve the character issue will be less. After all, the prize has been won. Added to that, the normal stresses of marriage will magnify any character disorders, making them even more difficult to manage.

Do not move forward in a relationship if you or your partner have any character issues that have not been fully addressed and overcome.

Beware, too, of subtle indiscretions that may indicate a pattern of dishonesty or disrespect. For instance, watch out for broken promises. If he says he will be at your place to pick you up at seven o'clock but doesn't show up until nine, that may be a slip-up or it may be a character issue. If the two of you have been planning for weeks to attend a big concert, but then at the last minute she suddenly says, "Something has come up, and I can't make it," you may be dealing with someone who will always choose a more enticing offer over you. If he implies that he was out looking for a new job all day, but you later discover that he was on the golf course for more than half the day—and "Oh, can you lend me a few bucks to pay for dinner tonight? I'll get it back to you next week"—you are probably dealing with a character issue. Certainly, plans change, interruptions happen, traffic jams cause delays, unexpected guests pop in from out of town, but what you are looking for is a pattern of inconsistency. Do these things happen only on rare occasions, or are you noticing an ever-expanding list of broken promises in your relationship?

Watch for signs of rudeness or lack of consideration. Observe carefully how your partner treats waiters or waitresses at a restaurant. If he or she is short, irrational, or disrespectful of someone in a serving capacity, you can be quite sure that same attitude will one day be aimed at you should you proceed with this relationship.

I've spent my life as a psychologist. I believe people can change for the better if they genuinely want to and are willing to do the tough work to see change happen. But I must confess, my prognosis for a character disorder offers little good news. Only three experiences seem to bring any real change to someone who has a long-standing character disorder—a stint in prison, serving in the military, or a deep spiritual transformation. The truth is, even with the help of one of those three experiences, the likelihood that a character disorder can be treated successfully is extremely low.

If you encounter a character disorder in your relationship, run—don't walk—away from that relationship as fast as you can. It will not get better with time; if it changes at all, it must change before you go one step farther in your relationship. If you are a deeply caring, empathetic sort of person, always trying to help "fix" somebody else, you must be especially aware. You may be tempted to think, *Oh, if I just stay with this person a little while longer, he's going to make it. She's going to change.* No, they won't. Not until they have to, and your involvement will probably deter any progress, and it just might destroy both your lives. Run for your life!

On the other hand, if you and your partner both display qualities of good character on a consistent basis—you both speak the truth in love, you are honest in all your personal and business dealings, you strive to live in a manner that is above reproach—you can be confident that you have one of the key building blocks to a solid foundation on which to build your relationship.

Good character is one of the primary keys to a great relationship. Let's look at some more screening dimensions, particularly one of the most important of all twenty-nine essential dimensions, emotional health.

CHAPTER 4

DIMENSION **2** | The Quality of Your Self-Conception

I WAS TALKING with my good friend and colleague Les Parrott about the qualities of a good relationship when Les asked me, "Neil, if you could offer one word of advice to someone who is about to be married, what would it be?"

Without a moment's hesitation, I replied, "Get yourself healthy before you get yourself married."

In this regard, I'm not talking about physical health, although we are well aware of the value of good nutrition and exercise nowadays. But the health I see as crucial for your relationship to survive and thrive is *emotional health*.

If you try to build intimacy with another person before you have done the hard work of getting *yourself* whole and healthy, all your relationships will become attempts to complete yourself. Moreover, if you are not healthy yourself, you will almost always attach yourself to another person in hopes of validating your self-worth. It's as if you are saying, "He (or she) seems to have it all together, so if I attach myself to him, I can be healthy because he makes up for all the things I am lacking in my emotional stability."

That's why the second essential dimension of a great relationship has to do with the quality of your self-conception and that of your partner. A person who has a good self-conception doesn't depend on anyone else to provide validation and meaning for life. He or she is strong enough to face life alone if necessary. He is prepared to deal with the ups and the downs, the good and the bad, the joys and the sorrows, and the harsh realities of life. All good emotional health starts right here—having a good self-concept. A good marriage demands that both partners know themselves well and, frankly, that they *like* being who they are. They feel good about themselves and rightfully so.

What are some signs that will help you spot an emotionally healthy or unhealthy person? For one thing, a healthy person will look you in the eyes while talking with you rather than looking at the floor, their hands, or somewhere else around the room. He or she can carry on a conversation without stressing about it; they can process your comments and respond to them. He will take turns in the conversation, allowing you to get your point across. She doesn't always have to be right and respects your differences of opinion. A person with a well-developed self-conception is not defensive or anxious, even if he or she disagrees with you. Nor does a healthy individual feel compelled to control the conversation by talking too much, too fast, or too loud. He listens intently as you speak. She operates in an unselfish manner. Basically, a person with a good self-conception is comfortable with who he or she is.

On the other hand, a person who has a poor self-conception may suffer unusual shyness, feelings of worthlessness, inadequacy, or insignificance; or the opposite, a person may attempt to cover a poor self-concept through unusually bombastic, boastful behavior, or exhibiting bullying characteristics. At the extremes, a poorly developed self-conception may lead to outbursts of anger, use of profuse profanity, temper tantrums, verbal tongue-lashings, or even domestic violence. Clearly, you do not want to be in a close relationship with someone who has a poor self-conception. And if your self-conception is deficient, you are not ready to be in a serious relationship.

"Hey, Doc, you're taking this too seriously," I can hear you saying. "We live in the real world, not an ivory tower. Nowadays everybody has self-esteem issues; we're all dysfunctional in one way or another, aren't we?"

NO! Most people that you meet every day are not dysfunctional. Sure, everyone has life issues with which they are dealing; most of us have endured pain and hurt in our pasts; many of us have emotional baggage that we must unpack and clean out, but for the most part, the vast majority of people in our society are relatively normal. Millions of people are well-adjusted, emotionally healthy, and functioning fine, and until you are one of those people, you are not ready to be married.

Over the years, I've counseled with thousands of individuals and couples in psychotherapy, and I have discovered a provocative truth. Most of those couples did not first and foremost have marriage problems; in almost every case, one or both of the partners had emotional problems that were magnified under the intense friction and heat that marriage produces. In many cases, the problem had been there for years, often long before the couple got married. It may have been covered by a thin veneer of charm or class or fun, but like a volcano seething below the surface, when the pressures began to build, it took just a small crack, and suddenly there was an explosion of hot, verbal venom and vitriol.

When you are evaluating emotional health, it's vital that you consider the health of both partners. "Well, I feel that I am fairly healthy, emotionally speaking," Marcy said when we talked about her possible engagement to Matthew. "I know that Matthew has some emotional problems to work out, but I feel sure we will do fine together." As much as I tried to convince her to forgo marriage until Matthew was on solid emotional ground, the couple went ahead, married, and almost immediately began to have problems.

Let me state this important point again: *The relationship between two people can be no healthier than the emotional health of the least healthy person.* If you and your partner know yourselves well and are happy with who you are, you can handle the daily challenges and stresses of life without too many issues. But if your self-esteem is fragile, or if your partner's self-conception is based on what sort of job he or she has or how much money he makes or what she looks like, your relationship will be susceptible to all sorts of emotional troubles.

Three Signs of Emotional Health

Les Parrott and I have discussed emotional health at great length. We are convinced that people with a good self-conception invariably possess three foundational qualities. They have a great sense of their own significance; they are unswervingly authentic to themselves; and they have developed a lifestyle of self-giving rather than self-seeking. How, then, do those traits contribute to finding your soul mate?

1. A PROFOUND SENSE OF SIGNIFICANCE   People who are emotionally healthy believe down deep at the core of themselves that they have great intrinsic value. They recognize that their value as a person is not based simply on what other people say about them, what they do for a living, their achievements or accomplishments, what neighborhood they live in, or other external factors. Their significance is *built in*; they believe they have been created with great value, and nothing life throws at them—not a breakup in a dating relationship, divorce, bankruptcy, being fired from a job, or experiencing other setbacks—can diminish their intrinsic value.

2. A LIFESTYLE OF UNSWERVING AUTHENTICITY—BE TRUE TO YOURSELF!   If the first sign of being emotionally healthy is having a sense of profound significance, the second sign is equally important. Simply put, you must develop a lifestyle of *unswerving authenticity*. In other words, emotionally healthy people are consistently true to who they really are deep inside, without reservation. Not only is this the best way for you to live, this sort of authentic living can truly liberate you and help you find the relationship of your dreams. In fact, if you don't get real with yourself, it is impossible to know your true soul mate. If you don't know who *you* are, how will you possibly know who he or she is who best matches you?

Many singles and newlyweds forgo their dreams so their partners can pursue their own dreams. While this sounds noble, and is for a while, far too many individuals have allowed somebody else to make those decisions for them and have lived to regret it. Stephanie had planned to be a schoolteacher, but midway through her college education, she met and fell in love with Jeremy. Stephanie dropped out of school to work as a bank teller so they could go ahead and get married; meanwhile, Jeremy would finish his master's degree. Of course, Jeremy never overtly requested Stephanie to make that sacrifice. He simply made it clear that he had to finish his schooling before they could get married. Consequently, Stephanie "decided" to put off her career out of love for her partner. "I'll go back to school after Jeremy is done with his education," she told her parents and everyone else who cautioned her against interrupting her academic pursuits.

Not surprisingly, a few months after the wedding, the couple discovered they were expecting a baby. Again, Stephanie's college education was put on hold. Another baby followed within two years. And then another. Today, more than twenty years later, Jeremy enjoys moderate success in his career, and Stephanie has yet to return to college. Her dreams have all but disappeared as she lives daily with regret. Although she enjoys being a mother, and she and Jeremy are still together, their marriage is tied together tenuously by mutual love for their children and not much more. Stephanie's mistake was not in loving her partner with a sacrificial love. She made the mistake of being untrue to herself.

3. AN ATTITUDE OF SELF-GIVING   When you know who you are, as a person of significance and authenticity, you are free to give love, kindness, compassion, patience, gentleness, or material possessions to other people with little or no thought of a return. Yet an amazing thing happens as you give of yourself; you will find that other people want to give back to you! There is something extremely contagious about being a giver rather than a taker. Once you master this quality of self-giving love, you begin to attract quality people. This makes sense since you are transcending your own boundaries, paying attention to other people's needs. When you do that, it is amazing how many people want to befriend you.

On the other hand, be careful if the person you are dating exhibits attitudes of selfishness. An emotionally healthy person will always have at least three qualities that are the natural result of unselfishness: (1) He or she will be *generous* with time, money, and resources. (2) He will be *truthful* almost to a fault, because an unselfish person hates to see even a hint of deceit. (3) She will be *kind*. True love always looks out for the dignity and well-being of the other person. It seeks to give rather than to take. If your partner is prone to putting his or her needs, wants, wishes, and desires ahead of yours, be careful. The "I want what I want when I want it" attitude is the exact opposite of self-giving.

THESE THREE ELEMENTS—developing your sense of significance, living authentically, and learning to be a giver rather than a taker—will be the keys to your well-developed self-concept, which is an absolute must if you hope to find a lifelong relationship with your soul mate. Moreover, when you find another person with whom you match in the majority of dimensions, and that person is emotionally healthy, you can proceed with tremendous confidence, knowing that you have already eliminated many of the main causes of divorce.

CHAPTER 5

DIMENSION **3** | Watch Out for Red Flags

ALTHOUGH WE ARE WATCHING for red flags in all of our dimensions, scanning for potential problems is such a crucial matter that it merits being one of the key twenty-nine variables that must be evaluated in a good relationship. Simply put, the third dimension is almost the opposite of the second—it is *the absence of emotional red flags*.

Have you ever been by the ocean on a day when the water is rough and choppy, and the undertow is downright dangerous? The lifeguards post red flags all along the beach, warning people to stay out of the water for their own safety. Anyone foolish enough to go in the water when red flags are flying does so at their own peril. They are just asking for trouble! The lifeguards will continue to fly the flags until the danger has passed and the sea is calm and safe to enjoy again.

In the realm of relationships, far too many people ignore the red warning flags, always at their own peril, which often involves a partner's pain as well. The red flags may signify the presence of a number of problems, but most often they warn of character disorders, addictions, or neuroses. My definition of an addiction may be more inclusive than some, but believe me, I have dealt with enough cases to recognize an addict. In my opinion, *any behavior that negatively affects your health, work, or primary relationships, yet you continue to engage in this behavior, is an addiction.*

Many people don't realize they need someone who is addiction-free if they hope to have a great marriage. Certainly few emotionally healthy people willingly choose to align their lives with a known drug abuser, but many people get married to people who have an addiction in one form or another. Some people drink too much or eat too much or too little; some people are addicted to pornography; others are addicted to nicotine, gambling, or prescription drugs; and many are addicted to "socially acceptable" drugs. Anyone who marries someone who is addicted to *anything* is asking for trouble.

One woman sat in my office with her fiancé and told me, "I know that Donny has been drinking too much lately. It's really been a problem. But Donny, you've promised, haven't you . . ." She paused and looked over at her future marriage partner. "You promised that once we get married, you're not going to drink anymore. Right?"

Naturally, Donny nodded his head in agreement.

How naive is that?

Of course Donny is going to drink after they get married. He'll probably drink more, rather than less, since he is no longer on his best behavior! The time to get Donny help with his drinking is before the wedding ring goes on the finger, not after.

If you see any addictions or other serious emotional problems in the person with whom you are contemplating a relationship, these are red flags. Please walk away from that relationship as quickly as you can! Allow at least a year *after* the emotional red flag problem has been cured before entering anything more than a platonic friendship with that person.

"But Chad is going to Alcoholics Anonymous now," Laura protested when I gave her some fatherly advice against proceeding in her relationship with her boyfriend. "I think he's going to be fine," she said.

"No, you don't know that, Laura," I cautioned. "An alcoholic's life is usually in grave danger for a lifetime, but if he hasn't had at least one year of functioning as a sober human being, you dare not get more involved with him. Are you so sure that Chad will never return to drinking that you are willing to risk your whole life on it?"

"I never thought of it that way," Laura admitted.

"Give him time. Help him all you can, but he has to learn to live addiction-free on his own, not depending on you or anyone else, before he is ready to enter into such a serious relationship."

All addictions take time to cure, so don't try to rush the process. If you don't take the time to deal with it before your marriage, you can be certain that the red flag problem will persist and will cost you dearly in time, money, and energy after you are married. I have never seen a good marriage involving one or both partners who had an untreated addiction of any kind. Certainly, I've seen a number of wonderful marriages in which a partner was a recovering alcoholic or a former drug addict. But without going through a stringent recovery process and establishing new "clean-living" patterns, it is almost impossible to have a happy, fulfilled, long-term relationship with someone who is addicted to alcohol, drugs, pornography, gambling, eating disorders, compulsive behaviors, or any other type of addiction.

Worse yet, most people with addictive personalities usually struggle with more than one addiction. For example, a person who is addicted to gambling is often addicted to alcohol or drugs as well.

How do you know if a person has an addiction? Remember, if they continue to engage in any behavior that negatively affects their health, work, or primary relationships, they have an addiction. Most addicts will adamantly declare that they can voluntarily quit the behavior any time they want. Don't believe them. Addicts become skilled liars and develop intricate webs of deceit to cover their addictive behavior. If you even suspect that your partner is involved in addictive behaviors, you should encourage him or her to seek professional help immediately, and protect yourself by not moving one inch farther into that relationship.

Say "No!" to Neuroses

Any indication of a neurosis is another red flag. We've all heard the term "neurotic," but what does it really mean? Basically a neurotic is a person who suffers from excessive anxiety that causes him to be incapable of handling the everyday challenges and frustrations of life. The neurotic's frantic efforts to manage this anxiety become major problem patterns in themselves. For instance, when anxiety is too high, he or she easily becomes depressed. Such depression is often the result of trying to shut down one's inner psychological systems to avoid experiencing the intense anxiety. But the clamping down causes an inner slump the neurotic person can't control, leading to even deeper depression.

When a person feels threatened by everyday events or problems, the response is often to avoid them, or to run from the problems rather than facing them. This usually leads to more problems. Their depression may be caused by a physical condition, but more often it is the result of anger, insecurity, guilt, shame, or an experience of loss. No wonder many divorced individuals experience extreme levels of depression and, conversely, no wonder so many untreated depression cases end up in divorce court. What a horribly vicious cycle!

Most types of neuroses can be treated with psychotherapy, and many people who have experienced even difficult neuroses have learned to manage them well and have gone on to live productive, healthy lives. But the time to treat any neurosis is before you enter a serious dating relationship.

There are all sorts of other red flags to watch for when you are considering someone for marriage. For example, some people are impulsive and want the relationship to proceed much too rapidly. "We have known each other now for two weeks, and we think we are great together, so why don't we just go ahead and get married?" Often, well-meaning, "hyper-spiritual" people slip into this error. "We know this is fast, but we are exceptionally well matched. God brought us together, so we're sure it is his will that we marry now."

I'm not going to argue with God, but a two-week courtship is too fast. Slow down; if the relationship is of premium quality, it will still be thriving six months from now.

Some people are too young to be getting married. More about that later, but for now, please understand, it is vital that people be old enough to know themselves well, at a deep level, before they start choosing the person they believe is the right mate for them for a lifetime. Too fast, too young, or too eager—these are all red flags that should caution you to slow down and take another look at this relationship.

Beware, too, of "boomerang" relationships, in which a person is trying to find the healing that he or she did not receive in a previous relationship. Too often, the person who has not taken the time to process what went wrong, to accept responsibility for his or her actions and attitudes, and make changes accordingly, is destined to repeat the problem all over again.

What freedom and joy it is to pursue a relationship when you know that all the red flags are gone. If you are not certain whether or not the flags are flying, ask people who know you and your partner to tell you the truth about what they see in your relationship. The seas should be calm and the sailing smooth. Only when you have established the absence of red flags with certainty is it wise to step into the relationship waters. Only then, with no red flags of warning, are you free to enjoy the natural beauty and warmth of a healthy relationship . . . assuming, of course, that you do well in the other twenty-eight essential dimensions!

CHAPTER 6

DIMENSION **4** | Anger Management

ANN AND JEFF had been meeting with me in premarital counseling for several weeks before they dropped the bomb. Sitting next to each other on the sofa in my office, holding hands and smiling at me, Ann and Jeff were the picture of a couple in love. Young, vibrantly alive, intelligent, and articulate, they seemed to have everything going for them. It didn't surprise me that they fidgeted nervously when I told them this session would be about resolving conflicts. That's when Ann hit me with the big one.

"But Dr. Warren," she said demurely, "Jeff and I never have any conflicts."

"Oh, really?" I asked, honestly amazed. "You never get angry with each other?"

"No sir, Dr. Warren," Jeff piped in. "As a matter of fact, Ann and I have never even had a fight!" Jeff leaned back on the couch with a pleased look on his face.

"Oh, that's too bad," I responded.

Jeff sat back up and leaned forward toward the coffee table as he spoke. "No, Dr. Warren. You must not have understood what I said. I said that Ann and I have never had a fight, not a single argument where we really got angry with one another."

"Really?" I asked.

"Really!" Ann chirped.

"I'm so sorry to hear that," I said.

The couple looked at me, then at each other, then back at me, as though they were wondering if they had somehow gotten off the elevator on the wrong floor and had stepped inside the wrong office for today's session. I could tell they were bewildered, so I continued. "You see, you probably aren't ready for marriage yet. If you have never had a fight, if you've never gotten angry with one another, if you've never had a conflict of some kind in which you disagreed with each other so adamantly that you really became upset, then you've probably never learned how to resolve conflicts in your relationship. And if a good marriage requires anything, it absolutely demands that you learn how to manage your anger and resolve conflicts."

Similar to many couples I've known in therapy over the years, Ann and Jeff assumed that the absence of anger was a real plus in their relationship. They truly believed that no conflict was better than having to resolve conflicts. But that is simply too idealistic. People do get angry in good marriages, and conflicts do occur. The wise couple will learn how to deal with conflicts *before* they get married, rather than wait for reality to burst their balloon of idealistic expectations the first time a disagreement occurs within the marriage. Certainly when anger leads to inappropriate behavior or a couple have so many conflicts that you wonder what they actually have in common, they may be too different from each other to create a great marriage and thrive in it. But in the best relationships I've seen over the years, one common element is nearly always evident—the couple have learned how to manage their anger without compromising their individual authenticity.

On the other hand, more marriages break up every year because two people do not know how to manage their anger in relation to each other than any other single reason. Obviously, how a couple handle anger and conflicts can literally make or break the relationship.

How Not to Manage Your Anger

It's important to understand that anger itself is not inherently evil. It is a natural emotional response that can propel human beings toward noble goals. Anger can help us to stand up for what is morally right and can cause us to oppose injustice, inequities, and oppressive behavior. But there is a big difference between anger and aggression.

Anger is a physiological response in your body to something that is wrong. Aggression is a destructive response to anger, lashing out in revenge, ridicule, and verbal or physical abuse. These responses are almost always wrong in themselves. But if you harness your anger, you will possess incredible power to right that which is wrong.

Handled correctly, anger can be a positive thing. Unfortunately, anger is more often mismanaged than managed well. One of the most common reactions to anger is *exploding*. If you (or your partner) frequently lose your temper, fly off the handle, give somebody a piece of your mind—or any other euphemism for "losing it"—you are an exploder. The threat of an angry explosion hangs over your relationship like the Sword of Damocles hanging by a thread above your head, waiting to drop. It may come in various forms, such as loud yelling, verbal bombshells, pounding a wall, spewing a litany of expletives or bitter put-downs, desk or counter pounding, face slapping or other expressions or threats of physical violence and aggression. Whether you are the perpetrator or the victim of such explosions, you have a problem, and you dare not even think about marriage until you find help and tame those expressions of unbridled anger.

A lesser known but equally as devastating anger-management technique is *somatizing*. Rather than lashing out at someone else, the person who somatizes his or her anger allows it to fester inside them as bitterness and resentment, constantly eating away at them like a cancer. The unresolved anger may cause all sorts of maladies in one's body, including headaches, stomachaches, colds caused by viruses that the body's normal antibodies are powerless to dispel, colitis, hypertension, heart attacks, and a variety of other physical problems. Basically, the unresolved anger causes the body's immune system to be weakened, making it more susceptible to attacks.

A third way of poorly handling anger is to *turn it inward* on yourself in some self-punishing way. Many people are their own worst enemies at this point. They beat up on their own self-image over and over again. They continually deliver angry messages to themselves. In some ways, this method of managing anger is more socially acceptable than others. We almost appreciate a person who reproaches himself regularly. It seems much kinder to vent your anger at yourself than at somebody else or a competitor.

People who turn their anger inward tend to look at what is wrong with life rather than what is right. They fret about the things that need fixing instead of the work that has been accomplished. Often an overwhelming sense of inadequacy and helplessness leads them into dark periods of depression. Thoughts of suicide are not uncommon for people who feel beaten down and seem to have little hope of seeing a change.

If you are contemplating marriage with someone who turns anger inward, please do not proceed in that relationship before you get help. Because depression and marriage are so incompatible, we realized at eHarmony early on that we must screen for depression in our personality profile questionnaire. We dared not even allow people who were depressed to get deeply involved with others prior to dealing with their condition. A depressed person is simply not ready for a dating or marriage relationship. That's not to say they cannot get help and enjoy a relationship in the future, but until they are emotionally healthy, they are like a bomb waiting to explode, causing pain for everyone else around them or imploding on themselves. In either case, you don't want to be romantically involved with such a person until they have been enjoying emotional health for at least a year.

The fourth common means of mishandling anger is what I call *underhanding*. A person may be extremely angry beneath the surface, but the anger is subtly expressed with humor or sarcasm in such a way that you feel the zing or the jab, and you are not sure whether you should laugh or be insulted. "Hey, I was just teasing!" he crows when caught. "What's the matter with you? Can't you take a joke?" Either that, or the underhander will slouch into the "poor, poor pitiful me's," because "nobody wants to play with me." Passive-aggressive behavior can usually be found somewhere in the underhander's repertoire. He won't fight with you; he'll simply withdraw, pour himself into sports or work, or even some community service—anything just to punish you for what he feels you said or did to him.

Most underhanders are fairly good actors. Be careful; the under-hander will pretend to be a good friend, but evidence will show that he continually has self-interest paramount in mind and will even work to stab you in the back or undermine your success if he thinks your interests are coming before his. If gossip, things she did to obstruct you from getting ahead, or other forms of sabotage keep showing up in your relationship, you are probably dealing with an underhander.

The underhander is sly though. His motto could easily be: "Don't get mad; get even." He rarely expresses his anger overtly but, be assured, it *will be* expressed. She may be more prone to pouting than punching. Pouters don't usually want to tell you about their anger; they just want to punish you for it by making your day (or life!) as miserable as theirs. The difficulty in dealing with an underhander, of course, is that you have a hard time telling when the anger is over—if ever. With an exploder, you may have to go around the house picking up the pieces, but at least you know that the storm has passed. The underhander does not offer that assurance. You can never be sure where or when he will zing you again, usually when you least expect it. Again, you don't want to be in a long-term relationship with an underhander. In fact, any of these poor anger-management techniques will create major problems in a marriage relationship. If either one of you has a history of anger mismanagement, you should seek the help of a professional counselor who can help you deal with it, but DO NOT proceed toward marriage until you have established new anger-management patterns.

Can Anger Really Be Managed?

The simple answer is yes, it can be. It *must* be or it will destroy your relationship. Every person can master his or her anger and find constructive ways of expressing it while eliminating the destructive patterns. The key to handling your anger is to develop a solid self-concept. And your self-esteem will be determined by the degree of unconditional love you experience. When you know you are loved with no strings attached, it can set you free to feel good about yourself. You no longer have to be or do anything to earn the right to be loved—and understanding that truth alone will do more to help you manage your anger than anything else in life. If you have a choice, stay away from conditional friends and lovers.

The important thing you must understand about anger is that it is almost always about a person's pain. It's about hurt, frustration, and fear. Anger is always a secondary emotion—it is a consequence of something else in the relationship. If a person is angry a lot, their pain is probably pressing on them somehow. That does not mean you should condone mismanaged anger; you simply must understand that the person is carrying around some heavy baggage you cannot see.

Comedian Phyllis Diller used to say, "Don't go to bed mad. Stay up and fight." That's not bad advice. You may not be able to solve every crisis before bedtime, but don't allow anger to bother you all night long. Not everything is worth getting all hyped up about, so choose your battle lines carefully. Ask yourself, *Is this really important? Does this matter merit a confrontation?* Simply put, don't sweat the small stuff! Let the little things go. But at the same time, be careful not to allow little things to build up. If you accumulate enough of those little irritants without ever addressing them, it's as if you continue to pump hot air into a balloon. It can stretch only so far before it explodes.

Aunt Mabel should have gone to prison at age seventy-seven, but the judge was lenient on Mabel because of her age. Her crime? She killed her husband, Harold, by hitting him over the head with a frying pan.

Throughout their marriage, Harold treated Mabel horribly. He incessantly insulted her, made fun of her, and regarded her as a servant for his convenience. Despite such awful treatment, Mabel remained loyal to Harold for more than fifty years.

One day Mabel was complaining to a neighbor about Harold's constant harassment. The neighbor innocuously answered, "Why, Mabel, if my husband ever said anything like that to me, I'd take the heaviest frying pan I have, and while he was sleeping at night, I'd whack him over the head with it."

The neighbor's idea piqued Mabel's interest. A few days later, Harold was at his ornery worst. All evening he continued to hurl abuse at Mabel, nitpicking about everything and anything: "The supper is cold"; "the house is a mess"; "this room is too hot." Each bit of his harangue stretched Mabel's patience a little farther beyond her limits.

The final blow came when Harold deliberately changed the channel on the television while Mabel was watching her favorite program. Mabel's blood began to boil.

"Harold, I am *going* to watch my story," Mabel said defiantly.

"Oh, yeah? Over my dead body!"

Harold shouldn't have said that.

Later that night, as soon as Harold began to snore, Mabel slipped into the kitchen, found the heaviest frying pan in the cupboard, and bashed in Harold's head. When she went to trial, the judge could not believe that the sweet little septuagenarian could possibly have been in her right mind when she split Harold's skull, so he ruled that she was too old and mentally incompetent to stand trial.

Mabel happily continued to watch whatever she wanted on television until she passed away at ninety-five years of age!

Did Mabel kill Harold over a television program? Of course not. But it was one little thing, built on another, until she couldn't take it any longer. Don't sweat the small stuff, but don't let the small stuff make you sweat, either. Confront your partner where it really matters, and seek to deal with anger before it deals with you.

CHAPTER 7

DIMENSION **5** | Obstreperousness

I'M LOOKING FOR someone who knows how to cut curly hair," Glen said as he sidled up to the receptionist's desk at the upscale hair-styling salon. "I'm new to town, and I've always had trouble finding someone who can tame this mess." Glen pushed his fingers through his long, curly blond mane. "I've discovered that not everyone who is a good stylist is good at dealing with these kinds of curls," the tall, handsome fellow said with a smile.

The receptionist was already busy searching the screens on her computer, looking for a stylist who might be available for a walk-in, and who might be adept at dealing with Glen's curls.

"I can do that for you," a voice said from off to the side of the counter. "I was married to a fellow for seventeen years who had hair just like yours. I did his hair all the time. You'd be no problem." The pretty stylist had been sitting behind the counter, taking a break, and had noticed Glen when he'd come in the salon. Now, she got up and extended a hand in Glen's direction. "I'm Alene. Come on, my chair is right back here."

Alene pointed Glen toward her workstation as she nodded to the receptionist. For the next hour, Alene washed Glen's hair, conditioned it, cut it, washed it again, styled it, blew it dry, and shaped it with gel. They carried on a conversation filled with lively banter during the entire hour. Every time Alene touched Glen's head or brushed by him, it was as though electric sparks flew between them in the salon. It was obvious that they were attracted to each other. Before he left that day, Glen tipped Alene generously and asked her out.

Alene looked around the salon furtively. "Call me at home," she said as she wrote her home number on the back of her salon business card.

Glen was glad to call her anywhere. He called her that night, and the two struck up an exciting relationship filled with fireworks from the beginning. Their dates ran the gamut, from camping trips along the Colorado River to attending formal theatrical productions, to ball games, to art shows. Glen loved it all. Formerly married to a rather dull, methodical homebody, Glen was awed by Alene's spontaneity and "I'll do anything that's legal" attitude. Alene loved to have fun and seemed to draw energy from their activities, producing a natural high.

But when the activities were done, Alene came down . . . hard. She lapsed into prolonged periods of moodiness, lashing out at Glen for no apparent reason. On several occasions, he left her house vowing never to return. But he always did.

Gripped by her beauty and excited by her vivacious and spontaneous side, Glen was equally baffled by the Alene he saw at times who seemed so foreign to the person with whom he had fallen in love. For instance, although Alene was meticulous about her makeup and immaculate in her dress, her house was almost always a mess. The dichotomy struck Glen as odd, but he enjoyed the way she looked and figured he could learn to live with her chaotic housekeeping.

More disconcerting to Glen were Alene's emotional swings. Some days Alene was so demanding and irritating, she was almost intolerable. But on other days, she was as sweet and charming as could be. But the more time Glen spent in close proximity to Alene, he saw more of her harsh, unattractive characteristics. Because he loved her, Glen attempted to pacify Alene, often making excuses to his friends and family members for her sometimes rude, often offensive behavior. He did everything he could to please her, but his best wasn't good enough. She walked out of his life into the arms of another man she had met at the salon.

At first Glen was devastated, but after the initial shock wore off and his heart had some time to heal, Glen realized that he had been lucky. He had been ready to buy Alene an engagement ring, but he had been blinded to her true character.

He poignantly said, "I tried everything I could to please her, but Alene is impossible to please."

Glen was absolutely correct. Had he been aware of the twenty-nine dimensions of a good relationship, the screening dimensions might have helped him avoid the heartache and saved him some time. All of the screening dimensions must be taken seriously if you hope to find your soul mate—or if you just want to avoid relationships that are unhealthy. But this dimension is one that you dare not underestimate.

What Is Obstreperousness?

One of the less frequently discussed dimensions that we include in our twenty-nine key traits to be considered is *obstreperousness*. That is a big word for a person who is harsh, critical, unappreciative, difficult to please, and never satisfied. You don't want to be married to an obstreperous person, no matter how much money he or she has or how great a lover he or she may be! An obstreperous person will drain you of every ounce of energy you have and will make life a living hell.

The colloquial meaning for *obstreperousness* is similar to that of someone feeling extremely uncomfortable within herself. She is miserable and no matter what you do, or how hard you try, you cannot make her happy. Whether you see obstreperousness in a man or a woman, it is not a pretty sight, and it definitely is not a quality you want to spend the rest of your life placating, tolerating, or combating.

Of all the screening categories, a critical attitude is one of the most damaging to a relationship. It will almost always destroy a marriage. The obstreperous person is quick to find fault (usually in somebody else) and quick to attribute blame and try to instill guilt. He is almost obsessed with proving the other person wrong and himself right. She is usually negative in her basic attitudes toward life.

You look at a beautiful sunrise and say, "What a gorgeous day!"

The obstreperous person looks at the same scene and says, "Yes, but it's raining . . . somewhere."

We all know people like that—negative, dour and sour, filled with self-pity or dragging around a victim's mentality, and basically not a whole lot of fun to be around. Why in the world would you ever want to be married to such a person?

The problem, of course, is that many obstreperous people are quite skilled in subtle trickery when it comes to masking their inner selves in the early stages of personal relationships. They may be strikingly pretty, as in Alene's case, or extremely creative and, at times, they can be quite friendly and cooperative, but don't be fooled. These are "players extraordinaire"! They are obsessed with getting what they want and will play you like a fine instrument if you let them, pressing all the right buttons, plucking all the right strings, to get where they want to go. But unfortunately, the obstreperous person doesn't really know where he wants to go in life or what he really wants. Why? Because she hovers precariously near the brink of a borderline personality disorder.

Shockingly, more than ten million people venture back and forth across that borderline in America every day. Dealing with a borderline personality disorder is so difficult, I refused to see people in therapy if I recognized them as borderlines. (Does that give you a hint what your response should be to one of these people?)

The reason I refused to waste their time or mine was because it is a no-win situation. Many obstreperous individuals are quite clever and extremely charming when you first meet them. But the closer you get and the more involved with them you become, the more you realize it is impossible to please such a person.

The first thing an obstreperous person will do is to compliment you: "Dr. Warren, you are so wonderful, and we have enjoyed coming to therapy with you."

(Watch out. If you look carefully, you can see the tennis ball hanging above the net, and the obstreperous person is about to slam it in your face!)

"Yes, we've been coming here for the last three months, and *we've paid you a lot of money*; I was just counting up in our checkbook last night how much we've paid you and, frankly, *our marriage is no better* now than when we first started coming! Harry is still doing a lot of drinking, and we still fight and fuss . . . Therapy just hasn't helped us."

"Yes, I think you are right," I might say. "I think we should call it quits."

"Call it quits!" the obstreperous person rails. "Are you kidding? After all the time and money we've invested in coming here to talk with you. Oh, no! We're not calling it quits. No, sir! Why, I can't believe that you want to back away from what is obviously a failure. You just want to stop now and walk away?"

"Eh, yes, I think we need to . . ."

"Nooooo! No way!"

"Well, all right, let's try to work on your relationship—"

"Yes, Doc! Let's do work on our relationship. I hope you have a better plan this time than you did last time, something different from what you've utilized so far because, as I say, that sure wasn't getting us anywhere. This hasn't worked at all!"

It's always somebody else's fault according to a borderline personality. If you detect a borderline personality, you can't get out of the way fast enough!

Borderline people will attempt to pull you into situations that you should never allow yourself to get into—situations just short of being unethical, immoral, illegal, or otherwise compromising.

"Dr. Warren, Harry and I were wondering if you and Mrs. Warren would come to our house for dinner on Friday night. We just love you so much, and we appreciate all that you have done for us. We'd like to express some of our thanks by having you as our guests."

All along, these are the people who will make accusations about you to a licensing board, an ethics committee, your boss, the Internal Revenue Service, or some higher authority when things fall apart for them—which they will. Many kind and well-intentioned leaders have been ruined by allowing an obstreperous person, or a person with a borderline personality disorder, to lure them into an unethical situation, only to have the borderline person turn around and use that same scenario to snare the leader in some sort of scandalous, often career-crushing activity.

Obstreperous people are in so much personal pain and are so vengeful, they will go after you with everything they can, and they will aim for the jugular. You do not want to be married to an obstreperous person. I have never known of a successful marriage in which one partner was obstreperous. One of the most intriguing books on this subject that I've read is *I Hate You—Don't Leave Me* by Jerold J. Kreisman and Hal Straus (New York: Avon Books, 1991). The title sums up the dilemma in which you will find yourself trapped if you continue a relationship with an obstreperous person.

My advice? Don't try to fix the obstreperous person; try to avoid such a person. Until he or she is willing to admit the problem and take steps to receive help in dealing with it, an obstreperous person will never make a good marriage partner. As much as it hurts, you must move on.

CHAPTER 8

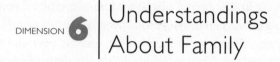

DIMENSION **6** | Understandings About Family

SOMEWHERE ABOUT MIDWAY through their first date, Sarah made up her mind that her first date with Ed would be her last. It wasn't that Ed wasn't a nice guy, or that he exhibited rude behavior, or that he was not good-looking or a great conversationalist. In fact, as Sarah mentally checked off similarities and differences in her mind, she and Ed matched up rather well. But as the conversation took a different turn, Sarah's heart took a dive. They were talking about Ed's rambunctious nephews when Ed nonchalantly said, "Whew! I don't think I could handle that. I don't ever want to have any children!"

Sarah wasn't sure she understood what he meant. Was it just that he didn't want undisciplined children such as his nephews, or did he not want children at all? When Sarah pressed him on it, Ed did not back down from his statement.

"No, I'm thirty-seven years old and extremely career-oriented," he said. "I just don't see children fitting into my life at this point."

Sarah quizzed him further, hoping that perhaps Ed had a short-term goal within his sights, something he was trying to accomplish, after which he would be more favorably inclined toward having children.

"Actually, I'm quite content," Ed said. "Sure, I'd like to be married. I want my wife to be able to travel with me to various parts of the world and do all the fun things neither of us have had the opportunity or the desire to do with anyone else. But I really don't want kids.

My brothers and sister all have children and I enjoy them, but I don't need kids to complete my life."

Sarah and Ed had a lovely dinner and a lively conversation. When he dropped her off at her home, Ed said, "I've really enjoyed our time together, Sarah, and I'd like to see you again. I have some tickets to the symphony concert in town next week. Would you be willing to join me?"

Sarah smiled at Ed and looked him directly in the eyes. She spoke softly, slowly, and distinctly: "Thank you so much for a delightful evening, Ed. I've enjoyed being with you. You are a wonderful person, and I really think we hit it off in a lot of ways. But no, I don't think we should go out again. I hope you know that you have many great qualities, but I'm looking for a certain person who matches up with my interests, desires, and long-term goals. Part of my dream is to have a home and a family, and that includes having babies. You've made it quite clear tonight that despite the strengths we both have, that is not part of your long-term plan. I understand that, and I hope you understand my decision not to waste your time or mine. I like you a lot, and I want the very best for you, as well as for me. Thank you, Ed. Good night."

With that, Sarah left Ed standing on the doorstep and moved on with her life. By recognizing the importance of a family to her and the obvious lack of interest on Ed's part in having a family, Sarah made the right decision. She also handled it extremely well, allowing Ed to maintain his dignity and minimizing any potential heartbreak that could have resulted had she accepted more dates with Ed knowing about his choice not to have children. Sarah's decision illustrates another of my favorite principles: The truth is always friendlier than anything less than the truth.

Choosing the right person to marry is already a large enough decision. When you add the possibility of bringing children into the world, you definitely want to make sure you both are on the same page. Kids don't disappear after a wild, wacky, wonderful weekend. (I know some parents of college students who are wondering if indeed their kids will ever leave home!) Children are there on Monday morning as well as Saturday nights. The sheer constancy of parenting requires a deep, strong, lasting commitment between a husband and a wife. That's why it is absolutely crucial for you to discuss in detail the idea of having children, with all of its ramifications, before you get involved in a serious dating relationship that could potentially lead to marriage.

The matter of having children can be confusing if you don't look at all aspects of the issue very carefully. Many singles like to play with children, to bounce them on their laps, to tussle with them on the floor, to push them on the swing set, to have fun with them . . . , and then to go home to peace and quiet. But often it's not enough merely to enjoy children for a few hours if you are considering this person for a long-term relationship. Many singles are looking for somebody who wants to have children, but have you considered whether this person is good with children? Does he or she possess a gentleness that is absolutely necessary with young children? Can this person provide firm but loving discipline, not simply playing a "Disney Dad," a parent who wants to be a friend to his children rather than a father?

If one person has a strong desire to have children and the other has little to no desire for kids, you may have a great friendship, but please do not get married, regardless of the number of other dimensions in which you may match. The "family" dimension is simply too all-encompassing for parents to be anything but perfectly matched. To have children or to not have children is only the beginning. How many children do you want to have? If one partner wants two children and the other partner wants five kids, you are going to have either a lot of stress or a lot of negotiating going on within that relationship. Then there are issues such as infertility, adoption, foster parenting, what sort of home environment you want for your kids, parenting styles, and acceptable methods of discipline, all of which you need to discuss thoroughly, clarify, and agree on *before* you are married.

The same care should be taken when you are considering a relationship in which you may be a stepparent, or the person you are interested in will be called on to be a stepparent to your child. In many ways, you must be even more attentive when looking at stepparenting possibilities. After all, it's one thing to be raising your own children; it is another matter entirely to be called on to be a mom or a dad to children who do not share your DNA.

Unquestionably, children can rock your world. Few experiences in life will call for more major changes in your lifestyle than having children. But babies are so cute and cuddly, who wouldn't want to have a baby?

Oh, a lot of men.

While many modern guys are much more sensitive, caring, and emotionally in touch with their inner feelings than men were encouraged to be in previous generations, most guys still tend to be more career-oriented than children-oriented. Sure, most guys will *tell* you they want a child, as long as a nanny comes with it! Whereas many women grow up looking forward to having children, most guys rarely give the issue much thought. Men may assume that they will one day reproduce, but few guys dwell on it or spend a great deal of time preparing for parenting. They figure they'll read a book or watch a video on the subject a week or two before the blessed event. Certainly there are exceptions, but you would do well to ask yourself, *Do I really want a baby with this person?* If you're still unclear about what's at stake, ask yourself, *Do I really want to have a* teenager *with this person?*

I occasionally have counseled women who did not want to have children, although that is less common than men who are indifferent about the matter. Sometimes a woman is forced into having children by a man who says, "If you're not going to have kids, then get out there and get a job." Certainly, if both parents are not wholeheartedly committed to the task of having a child and raising that child to adulthood, they should not have a baby. And if one partner wants children and the other does not, those two individuals must consider the possibility that they are not well matched to each other.

Having children is rarely the sole cause of marital problems; the pressures of having a baby and raising a family simply exacerbate whatever is already happening in the relationship, positively or negatively. If there are fissures or cracks in the relationship, the additional stress of raising kids will break them wide open. One thing is certain:

It is naive to think your relationship with your partner won't change when you have kids. It will and you should expect that. You must recognize that trade-offs are inevitable. Simply stated, unless you have hired help and lots of it, you will not be able to function in the same free and easy manner you did before the children came along. You won't be able to go to some places or do certain things. On the other hand, plunging into normal everyday kid-oriented activities will throw you out of sync with most of your single friends, relatives, or childless colleagues and peers. Parenting involves playgrounds, booster shots, cartoon-character-themed birthday parties, piano lessons, Little League games, and a whole lot more. It is simply impossible for you and your partner to give each other the same amount of attention you did before the kids came along . . . but maybe that's not so bad.

Most of us have a tendency to be selfish, even in a well-matched, mutually satisfying relationship. Yet nothing in life will teach you how to surrender your rights in sacrificial love more than having children. If you or your partner is not up for that kind of sacrifice, you should reconsider your relationship or reconsider the issue of having a family.

After your spouse, your children should be your number one relationship in life. You'll have them, at best, for only a short time. At times you may feel you can't wait until they are grown up and gone, but ask any parent of college- or career-aged kids and they will tell you, "The years just whisked right by and before I knew it, my tiny tot was a teenager, then out of school and out on his own. It all seems like yesterday . . ."

No question about it, if life were a tennis game, having children would be break point . . . but it is also advantage: love.

CHAPTER 9

DIMENSION **7** | Family Background

THE SEVENTH SCREENING DIMENSION is related to the sixth, in the sense that you need to be on the lookout for any signs indicating that your partner's family background has been unhealthy, warped, or dysfunctional in any way. Certainly, if one or both of you have been raised in a dysfunctional family, it doesn't disqualify you from marriage, but you must make sure that the impact of your upbringing in that family has been recognized and worked through. Why? Because dysfunctional families breed dysfunctional families. Unless you want to perpetuate that cycle, you must be able to see consistent, adequate evidence that you and your partner are free from the ball and chain of any past dysfunctionality in one or both of your families.

In marriage, whether you like it or not, you don't marry merely an individual, you marry the entire family! Get to know your partner's family members, or learn as much about them as you can at the earliest juncture possible. Nowadays, it is not uncommon at all for a bride and a groom to meet each other's family members at the wedding rehearsal dinner! Whew! That is too late to detect latent dysfunctionality that may permeate the whole clan.

Perhaps no other area of a couple's relationship can create such emotional trauma as stress between or about each other's families. Like it or not, your family has been and will continue to be important to you—and your spouse probably feels the same way about his or her family. All well and good, until relatives—regardless of their intentions—try to intervene or control your relationship with your potential marriage partner. Getting into a marital relationship with somebody who has a very controlling parent can be a major problem for a marriage. That's when in-laws can become outlaws.

Why is uneasiness about family backgrounds so common? Let's face it: Your attachment to your parents and siblings may appear to be much stronger than your ties to your prospective marriage partner. After all, you grew up in your parents' home, you spent some of the most important years of your life under their watchful eyes. In most cases, part of you still wants to please them by maintaining family loyalties. That's why there is so much truth to the old saying: "In every marriage, there are at least six people—the wife, the husband, and the two parents of each" (even if the parents are deceased).

When anything threatens your relationship with your family, you automatically recoil. If your partner says something critical about your relatives, you are personally offended. At the same time, you may purposely avoid becoming close to your partner's family for fear that getting along too well with your potential in-laws may be perceived as disloyalty by your own relatives. It seems that either way you go, you lose. But it doesn't have to be that way.

From your parents' and your potential in-laws' perspective, your relationship presents a different set of problems. You often hear the phrase at weddings, "I didn't lose a daughter; I gained a son" (or vice versa). In many cases, parents and in-laws are quick to state this obligatory platitude but mighty slow to believe it! I know I was reluctant to "give away" Marylyn's and my three daughters, Lorrie, Luann, and Lindsay, on their respective wedding days, even though I believed that each of them was marrying a fine gentleman who would be a great husband.

When the minister asked the question "Who gives this woman to be married?" I wanted to shout out, "Nobody does! I want her to come back home with Marylyn and me!" Of course, I didn't, and our daughters are all happily married today, but the truth is, you will always be your parents' little girl or boy. Similarly, to some extent, your spouse will always be an outsider to your parents, as you will be to your partner's parents.

It is understandable if your parents are supersensitive about and overcritical of your partner. It may take them some time to appreciate the qualities in him or her that are quite obvious to you. Likewise, as a potential son-in-law or daughter-in-law, you will initially pose a threat to your partner's family members. You are the one who is trying to "steal" their baby from them.

What are some things you can do to help determine whether your relationship can withstand the pressures exerted by your family backgrounds?

1. *Study your potential partner's family.* After all, these people have had a great impact on the person to whom you are contemplating marriage, whether or not one or both of you downplay that influence. You might learn some significant things about your partner if you will take the time and effort to study his or her parents and siblings. Ask to see old family photographs, high school or college yearbooks, family wedding albums, or anything else that will provide clues to your partner's family background.

Ask your potential partner's parents about their family tree. Who were the first family members to come to this country? How did they get here; what did they do for a living; what were their religious influences and educational backgrounds? Listen carefully for hints that help you to understand the rationale and motives for their actions. You may never become best friends with your partner's family members, but you might discover some common ground between you— or not!

2. *Share your feelings about each other's families honestly but sensitively.* Remember, for better or worse, these people are still your partner's family members. If they rub you the wrong way, you mustn't hide that fact from your partner. Share your feelings honestly. But, as always, the key is to focus on your feelings rather than on what you think your partner's family member has done "wrong." Rather than saying, "Your sisters are rude, ignorant snobs," you might try saying, "When your sisters whisper to you around me, I feel that they are purposely trying to exclude me from the conversation."

Timing and privacy are also important when discussing family members. The best policy is: Never *criticize* your partner's family with respect and basic consideration. By doing so, you will remove or reduce a major source of parental intrusiveness and competitiveness that has created stumbling blocks for more than a few couples.

Remember, your goal throughout this process is to determine whether or not your "future in-laws" will be positive influences and, frankly, whether the two of you can handle living as part of each other's families. If you decide that you and your partner are well matched but your families are not, then you must determine whether you will be able to manage those family relationships effectively.

Invite Your Family's Opinions

The flip side to what you see in your partner's family is what your family sees in you and your partner's relationship. On a couple's wedding day, it is ideal when their family and friends are gathered to celebrate the joining together of two wonderfully matched individuals.

It is important for every man and woman to have both of their families and friends expressing positive things about the marriage, such as, "Oh, I'm so happy for them! This is just the greatest thing. My close friend Kathy is getting married to Brian, and we just think that Brian is wonderful for her." If possible, you want your family and friends to be sitting there in the front rows at your wedding, their eyes sparkling with excitement. You want your family members and your partner's family members to be thrilled for you!

But what if your family thinks the person you are interested in is wrong for you?

Carly came to see me, and the moment she walked into my office, I could guess what had happened. She looked troubled, her countenance crestfallen. "My dad doesn't think that Andrew is right for me," she said with her face in her hands once we had closed the door. "I had hoped that my family would accept Andrew and love him like they love me, and that he'd love them like I love them. But my dad doesn't like him."

When your family does not approve of the person you are considering for a serious, long-term relationship, it does two things: First, it members to him or her. Rarely will anything constructive come from your critical comments. That doesn't mean you should pretend you don't notice things that bother you; just be wise in how you broach the subject. Even if your partner makes negative remarks about his or her parents or family members, don't you do it. Instead, point out the positive; accentuate their strengths rather than their weaknesses. Encourage your partner to honor his or her parents, and you may be surprised when that response is reciprocated toward your parents. But if that is impractical or impossible, at least hold yourself to this one: Keep it private! Never speak negatively about your partner or any of your partner's family members in front of his or her parents or yours. Wait until an opportunity arises when you and your partner can discuss the matter privately.

3. *Show both of your families that you care about them.* The key word here is *both.* While you don't need to treat each family member identically, equal treatment is usually appreciated. Let both families know that you have no intention of cutting yourselves off from them, but at the same time, let them know that if you do indeed go ahead and get married, your priorities in life will change. If or when you say, "I do," your prime allegiances immediately will transfer from your parents (or even yourselves) to each other. The commitment you make in marriage supersedes your loyalties to parents and siblings, and you will not feel disloyal or ungrateful about shifting your allegiance to your spouse.

But let both families know that just because in the future you may be spending less time with them and more time with your partner, your love, honor, and respect for your family members remain strong. You can express that devotion to your potential family members by sending them an occasional greeting card, telephoning or e-mailing, remembering birthdays and anniversaries, and, most of all, by visiting. Keep in mind the key word: *both.* If you live far from your families and visit or telephone one set of parents frequently, you should try to do the same for the other set of parents as well.

"That's silly!" some might say. Perhaps so, but if your goal is to get along with both sets of family members, it is wise to treat them all raises questions that perhaps you are not doing the right thing. Second, some individuals say, "If my family feels this way about this person that I love, well, forget them." Obviously, this attitude creates schism within the family relationships.

When someone such as Carly comes to see me because of family concerns, the first thing I do is seek to learn the truth about the relationship, why her dad feels the way he does. Remember, the truth will always be friendlier in the long run than anything less than the truth. If the parents have a good hold on the truth, we want to know it. As Carly put it, "I don't want to be married for fifteen years and have three kids, and then find out that my folks were right and wish that I had listened to them. I don't want to find the truth out a long time from now. I want to find it out now."

The second principle I propose is: Everybody's feelings and thoughts about your potential choice of a marriage partner are important for you to know. As I told Carly, "Whatever the feedback is, invite your family members to tell you. You want to hear what your dad thinks about Andrew." And you don't want to make Dad feel badly if he doesn't see things the way you do. Simply say, "Dad, I want to hear what you have to say. What do you think and feel about this person that I am thinking about marrying?"

The third principle I emphasized to Carly was, "Your choice is always law. In other words, whatever it is that you end up thinking or feeling, it is your decision that counts. Your dad doesn't make the decision about whom you will marry, nor does your mother. Nor does your uncle Jim or anybody else. *You* make the final decision. You have all the power—remember that. But also remember that you may have some blind spots. You may have a lack of perspective, and someone else close to you may have an ability to see better than you can. It is important that you get all the information other people have so you can make your decision with a lack of anxiety."

A good decision about a marriage partner is one that is good today, a month from now, ten years from now, and is still good on your twenty-fifth or fiftieth anniversary.

Maybe Carly's dad has some legitimate concerns. He says, "I don't think Carly should be marrying Andrew because Andrew doesn't have a good job. He doesn't seem to be able to provide a living for her."

"What else is it, Mr. Brown, that concerns you about Carly marrying this man?" I ask.

"He comes from a family I don't respect," says Carly's dad. "They don't seem to work hard. In fact, Andrew's dad doesn't seem to be able to hold a job, either." One by one, we will work through Carly's dad's concerns, and then I address them with Carly.

"Is there truth to the fact that Andrew doesn't have a good job?"

"Oh, my dad wouldn't be happy with anyone I wanted to marry," Carly says.

"Maybe so, but there is truth in the importance of having a good job to be able to support a marriage over time."

I am not going to let Carly make that unimportant by simply saying, "Dad wouldn't be happy with anybody." I want to get that out on the table to see if that's important. I want to go over those things one by one. If it becomes obvious to Carly that her dad has a point, she needs to face up to it. The truth is always friendlier than anything less than the truth.

On the other hand, if I think that Mr. Brown is indeed finding it difficult to let his daughter get married to anybody, then I'll ask if I can meet with Mr. Brown by himself. I will bring him in and ask, "Tell me, who is Carly for you?"

Mr. Brown says, "Carly is the most important person in the world to me. Her mom and I have had difficulty in making things work, but Carly has been an angel to me. I love her to the very depths of my being."

"It sounds as though Carly is really a major figure in your life. Does it concern you that she will become a less important figure in your life if she is married?" At some point, Mr. Brown recognizes the fact that Carly's marrying Andrew is not the problem for him. The problem for him is that Carly is getting married at all. He fears losing her.

If, indeed, Mr. Brown has some important reasons why Carly should go slow in making her decision about this man, I want to help Carly recognize them, not merely because her dad says so but because that is in her long-term best interests. But if he doesn't have any good reasons, then I want to help Mr. Brown resolve his issues about losing Carly in a way that doesn't affect her relationship with Andrew.

If your family expresses concerns about the person you are considering as a potential marriage partner, find somebody with whom you can talk it through. It may be a minister, priest, rabbi, or a professional marriage counselor, but find a person who brings some objectivity to the situation, not a blood relative or your best friend. You want somebody that is bright and insightful and can in a simple, nondefensive way call for the information, get it out on the table, and say, "Now, let's talk about what this issue means."

"What if my family likes the person more than I do?" you may ask.

In that case, be very careful. You are the one making the crucial decision. You must make it well. I know of a wedding a few years ago in which the bride and groom mutually decided at the last minute that they didn't want to go through with it. But they were both feeling pressure from their families. All the relatives and friends had come in from out of town, the band and the building had been reserved for the reception, and all the other myriad details that go into planning a wedding nowadays were in place. Just before the wedding was scheduled to begin, the couple announced that they had decided to postpone getting married. But rather than having everyone leave disappointed and feeling sorry for them, the couple invited their guests to the reception hall, where they decided to have a party "in celebration of a good decision." That took courage, but it was the best thing they could have done.

If you are walking down the aisle at your wedding and you suddenly realize, *This isn't right for me*, stop! Regardless of the cost, embarrassment, or anything else, it is not worth going through with a marriage to someone unless you are 100 percent convinced that you are well matched. Even if you are standing in front of a minister, priest, rabbi, or justice of the peace, whisper in the ear of the officiating person, "I feel badly about this, but I would appreciate your making my apologies known. I just don't think it is right for us to continue."

Before you take your vows, you are totally free, so if you sense any red flags or inner turmoil at the thought of marrying this person, understand that to proceed further would be the epitome of foolishness. But once you take your vows, you have a responsibility to honor them with a commitment for a lifetime. And that, of course, is why it is so important for you to be convinced that you and your partner are well matched long before you begin to walk down the aisle at your wedding.

GROUP 2

The Core Personal Dimensions

A SON WAS TALKING with his father about a woman the son was considering as a potential marriage partner. "Isn't she great, Dad? She's so beautiful, and she really motivates me to better myself."

"Yes, I can see that she's very attractive," the father said, stroking his chin, "and I'm sure she can be quite motivating . . . but she seems a bit selfish. Have you noticed that she always wants to do what she wants, and doesn't seem to be interested in what everyone else would like?"

"Oh, yeah, Dad, but she's really flexible. I can talk her into seeing things my way."

"I noticed that she doesn't like to be inconvenienced, either."

"Oh, I know, Dad. But she has a really great attitude. Don't worry, after we're married, she'll change."

The father looked his son straight in the eyes and said, "Yes, son, people change, but not much."

The father was more right than the son realized. That's why the second group of the twenty-nine dimensions you must consider about a relationship comprises what we call the "Core Personal Dimensions." These are sixteen characteristics of a person that are relatively difficult to alter. Some of them are genetic and have been established at birth; others have been ingrained by each person's environment and educational experience. Regardless, these dimensions are difficult to change, so it is vital that you and your potential partner evaluate these qualities very carefully. Remember, people change, but not much.

CHAPTER 10

DIMENSION **8** | Intellect

THE FIRST OF THE core dimensions is intellect. By intellect, I do not mean education (we'll look at that below), because it is possible to be extremely intelligent without having a formal academic education. Interestingly, there is no clinical or empirical evidence proving that two people will fare better in marriage if they are extremely smart. Nor is there evidence that a couple will do poorly in marriage if they are "not so bright." What does matter immensely is that the partners possess intellectual levels that are near the same. If one partner has a high intelligence quotient and the other partner's IQ is substantially lower, the couple are likely to be miserable together, regardless of how many other good traits they may have.

My own mom and dad fell victim to this disparity in intelligence levels. Of course, back then nobody was talking about how to be well matched, much less emphasizing that to be happily married you must be close to the same intelligence level as your spouse. Although my dad went to school only through the eighth grade, he was extremely bright, much brighter than I am and, unfortunately, much brighter than my mom.

Dad married Mom on the rebound. My dad's father was a minister in the same little country church where my mom and her family attended. Mom's dad was a leading layperson in the congregation.

Dad had been dating one of the more notorious young ladies of the community for a period when his older brothers confronted him with a warning: "You're going to get in deep trouble if you continue cavorting with that young woman!" Dad was a good man with high moral integrity, and he respected his brothers' opinions, so he broke off the relationship with the young woman for whom he cared deeply. Before long, he struck up a relationship with my mom, an attractive, sweet, simple girl down at the church. It was a safe marriage for my dad, so he no doubt never even thought about how important intelligence could be in a marriage. Nor did he consider how compromised life would be if he married someone who was not his intellectual match. He was nineteen years of age, and Mom was seventeen.

Amazingly, they remained married for seventy years! But for seventy years, they experienced the consequences of being mismatched intellectually. They seldom talked beyond the obligatory "How was your day?" type of questions. They had difficulty discussing the important events of the day, or even the deeper tenets of the religious faith they shared. Although they loved each other and were irrevocably committed to each other, their conversations were limited to mundane, everyday things. This is fine if it's the level on which you and your partner want to communicate. But when you run much more deeply, and your partner is not able to go there with you, it can be a frustrating experience for both of you.

In my own life, as I think back on the young women I dated prior to falling in love with Marylyn, they were all highly intelligent, as is Marylyn. I didn't consciously think, *Mmm, let's see, which of these women would be extremely bright?* Like most young men my age, I was looking for someone with an attractive appearance and a vivacious personality. I didn't sit down and calculate which young women would be closest to my intelligence, but I can't help wonder if on some level, because of what I had witnessed in my mom and dad's relationship, I knew deep inside that I did not want to marry somebody with whom I would have a discrepancy in levels of intelligence.

Obviously, this is not a dimension you can change. Oh, sure, you can study hard, educate yourself by reading books and take advantage of educational opportunities, but your basic intelligence is part of the package of genes you inherited from your parents.

Certainly, there are a half dozen or more types of intelligence that can be tested and measured. Intelligence quotient really has to do with neural circuits in a person's brain. It relates to the ability to grasp new information, how rapidly the mind functions, how well ideas are conceptualized and information stored in the mind. Some people have everyday, commonsense intelligence, and some people have "street smarts." But for the purpose of determining whether you and another person match in the area of intelligence, you need to think in terms of intelligence that you can usually pick up in a conversation.

I used to have a hobby—well, actually it was sort of a continuing education training experience for me—in which I would attempt to estimate the intelligence level of a person who had come in for their first psychotherapy session. I would secretly guess their IQ simply by talking with them. I would do this before giving any personality tests or formal intelligence tests. Then I'd administer a battery of standard tests, such as the Wexler Adult Intelligence Scale.

When I'd compare what I had estimated the person's intelligence to be with the actual level at which they tested, I'd usually come within ten points of the person's intelligence level, or what is known as "one standard deviation" on the Wexler scale. The "mean" score on the Wexler is 100, so if a person scores 100, he or she is right in the center of the distribution of scores. If he or she scores 130, that person would be in the top 1 percent of the most intelligent people who have taken the test.

Over the years of my clinical therapy, after dealing with thousands of people, I came to the conclusion that the individuals who were best matched for marriage nearly always came within ten points, or one standard deviation, of each other on the Wexler scale. In other words, their intelligence levels were very similar. It didn't matter whether they were a 70 on the scale or a 110, what mattered was that if he was a 70, she needed to be between 60 and 80; or if she were a 110, he needed to be between 100 and 120. Anything beyond that ten-point differential inevitably spelled trouble in the relationship.

Of course, I didn't have that information when Marylyn and I got married. We knew so little about how to choose a marriage partner; we had no idea that the best marriages are between people of similar intelligence levels. Then, one day while I was working on my doctorate at the University of Chicago as part of my class work, I had to administer several batteries of tests. Marylyn agreed to be one of my test cases, and one of the tests I gave her was the Wexler Adult Intelligence Scale. She scored slightly higher than I did! As I said earlier, Marylyn and I were simply lucky. Had there been a major difference in our intelligence levels, we'd probably not be nearly as happy in our marriage as we have been all these years.

But you don't need to run your potential partner through a battery of tests to tell if he or she is more or less intelligent than you are (although that wouldn't be a bad idea!). You can usually tell from a conversation if you are in the same ballpark intellectually. If a person is not as mentally quick as you, or doesn't seem to have a similar capacity to process information during a conversation, watch out! If you go ahead and marry this person, you could be condemning yourself to a lifetime of communication problems, boredom, or both.

Please understand, it is not a matter of how smart you are or how smart your partner is. There are as many people who score 70 on the Wexler scale as there are who score 130. What is crucial, however, is that you match closely in intelligence levels.

One of the difficulties for us at eHarmony is to match someone at either end of the scale. If you are a 130, you need a person who scores at least 120. But most of the world's population—about 95 percent—scores 120 or less on the Wexler scale. Simply by examining one category, you must rule out 95 percent of the world's population. Talk about a tough match!

Similarly, if you or your partner is on the other end of the scale, it is equally as difficult to find a match. But to enter a relationship with someone with whom you are not closely matched intellectually spells complications.

Some people try to play a little loose with the truth of this finding. "Oh, we're just a little more than ten points apart," Pete said when he discovered that he and Maria were fifteen points apart on the intelligence scales. "Surely, five points won't make a difference!"

But when I showed Pete the difference between 100 and 115, he was shocked. The person with a score of 100 may be a fine individual, but his or her ability to process information is radically different from the ability of the person whose IQ is in the 115 range. Can they go ahead and get married? Sure! Can they expect to be happy? Sure, about as happy as my mom and dad were . . .

My parents stayed together all those years because they had many things in common, and that is admirable. But if you merely stay together and yet are never truly able to communicate at a deep level with your spouse, is that a satisfying relationship? Is that the sort of marriage you want? I noticed as I was growing up that my mom was depressed quite frequently. And my dad immersed himself in his work and in serving at the church. I can't help but wonder if that's how they coped with their lack of intellectual similarities.

Surely, if my parents were living in that sort of forced incommunicado today, they'd be likely candidates for divorce or an affair. All too often, an intellectually mismatched man or woman with an otherwise wonderful spouse at home gets caught up in a dalliance at work when someone pays attention to how intelligent he or she is. "It wasn't about sex," Lindsey said. "I could talk to Stu (her friend at work) about business, current events, things happening in the world that mattered, and he comprehended and could relate. My husband's only interest in the newspaper was in reading the sports section."

Another common problem created by intellectual imbalances in marriage is that either one partner talks down to the other, or one partner is too intellectually intimidated to ever voice a contrary opinion or stand up for himself or herself.

Dan is a woodworker, and a good one, too. His wife, Jessica, is an interior designer with an extremely keen mind. While at first they were attracted to each other by their shared creativity, it soon became obvious that Jessica regarded Dan's work as menial labor, and she spoke of it that way. Worse yet, when she speaks of issues with which she is grappling in her work, she often tends to say something such as, "Oh, never mind, Dan. You wouldn't understand." Even when they watch the evening news together, Jessica feels compelled to explain the various nuances of the news coverage to her husband. Does Dan appreciate her comments? Not for a moment.

But Dan knows that Jessica can run rings around him intellectually. She can paint a picture with her words that traps him in a corner until she says the paint is dry and he can come out. So, rather than contest Jessica's opinions, Dan quietly retreats to his wood shop.

To avoid setting yourself up for that kind of misery, determine as best you can how well matched you are in the realm of intellect. If at all possible, it would be worth your investment to secure the services of a qualified therapist to administer some basic IQ tests to you and your partner. Make it a fun activity, a valuable learning tool, rather than a threatening experience. But take the results seriously.

If your scores are similar, rejoice and move on to examine your relationship in regard to the other dimensions. If your scores are greatly dissimilar and you and your partner are not in the same league intellectually . . . What was that I said about the truth always being friendlier than anything less than the truth?

CHAPTER 11

DIMENSION **9** | Similar Energy Levels

Early in my career as a psychotherapist, I began to notice a common malady among married couples who were having troubles in their relationships. One of the partners would have a boatload of energy; the other hardly had enough to get out of the chair and crawl to bed. On the other hand, I noticed that marriages in which both partners had similar energy levels seemed to be more successful.

Josh loves going full tilt all day long, working a full shift, then coming home and going out to play golf or playing on the church softball team. He will get up early on Saturday morning to wash his car, then head for the lake to spend the day water-skiing or riding a wave runner. Whatever sport is in season, Josh is out on the playground picking up a game with some of the local teenagers. And he keeps up with them well, even though Josh is more than twice their age.

Bethany is a homebody. She loves coming home from work, having a quiet dinner, taking her evening bath, and then relaxing in front of the fireplace to read a book or watch a movie. To her, exercise is nearly a dirty word! Although she will occasionally accompany Josh to one of his games or recreational activities, she rarely participates. She's much more likely to sit in the back of the boat and work on her tan than she is to don a pair of skis and skim across the lake. Often when Josh will come by the house in the evening and want to go out, Bethany will whine, "I'm too tired, Josh. If you want to go, fine; go ahead. Call me when you get home."

Clearly, if Josh and Bethany get married as they are contemplating, they will let themselves in for some major problems. Any time one person has a lot of energy and the other person has little, the satisfaction of both partners is reduced drastically in the marriage.

People will frequently contest this point with me. "Can't our energy differences be complementary?" Sheila wanted to know. "Austin doesn't have a lot of energy, but I do. Won't we balance each other out?"

I just haven't seen that to be the case. Yes, if everything else in the relationship is fantastic, I suppose you could tolerate a lack of energy on your partner's part; or the contrary, you may be able to tolerate that constant going, going, going. But if anything else is out of whack in the other dimensions, the energy issue will rear its head. It may show up in a variety of ways and locations—it may show up in your sexual relationship where one partner is ready for sex at the slightest encouragement while the other partner says, "Not tonight, sweetheart. I'm too tired."

It may show up in the way you share the workload around the house. In every marriage, there are all sorts of basic chores to be done—everything from taking out the garbage to scrubbing the bathtub, doing the grocery shopping, waiting for the cable TV repair person, doing the laundry, and perhaps the most delicate question in marriage: "Who's going to clean the commode?"

If she has a long list of household chores and projects that she wants to get done around the house, but he wants to spend Saturday afternoon on the couch watching college football because he is too tired to take on another project, you can be sure there is going to be tension around that home.

Similarly, if his idea of a romantic evening is to go out dancing till dawn, and your idea of a romantic evening is to stay home and watch television, don't be surprised if the romance reduces quickly in your relationship.

As with intelligence, it is not the amount of energy two people have that makes the difference. Two low-energy individuals can get along just fine and be perfectly content, as long as the other areas of their relationship are solid. In the same manner, two high-energy individuals can have a great relationship. It is when two people have radically different amounts of emotional energy that the disparities lead to problems.

Certainly, for some people the amount of emotional energy they exhibit is reflective of their poor physical health. They do not maintain a nutritional diet or they are grossly overweight. Perhaps they are not ingesting proper vitamins and therefore are lethargic. For others, their low energy can be traced to poor emotional health. Ann Marie lies around on the couch all day, apparently too tired to get out and do something. In reality, Ann Marie is deeply depressed and needs serious help simply to function in society.

Just the opposite, Mark cannot possibly stay still for more than a few minutes. He is so hyper, he has to be doing something every hour of the day until he finally runs out of steam around midnight. Clearly, neither Ann Marie nor Mark is ready for a serious relationship with anyone and especially with each other.

Still others simply operate on low wattage. They seem to drag their heels through life, never in a hurry, never highly motivated to do much of anything. "Let me sit down for just a moment," he says, "and see what's on the tube." He looks around for his best friend in life—the remote control. "I need to take a break," she often says. Again, this isn't necessarily a bad quality, unless you are pursuing a relationship with someone who has a high level of energy. Then it is a divorce waiting to happen.

Few counselors or religious leaders ever bring up the matter of similar energy levels as being vital to a great relationship, but common sense tells us that you want to be married to somebody who is very similar to you in this practical area.

CHAPTER 12

DIMENSION **10** | Spirituality

PERHAPS IN NO AREA is it more crucial to be well matched than in the area of spirituality. You may think it odd that spirituality is included among those traits that are relatively difficult to change, especially when it seems so much of modern religion tends to focus on conversion, change from one spiritual state to another. But understand, in the context of determining whether or not you match with a person well enough to consider marriage, spirituality and the depth of a person's faith in God are not necessarily the same thing. Of course they can be, but you will also find extremely "spiritually oriented" people who are agnostics and possibly even a few who are atheists, yet they consider themselves to be spiritual and, in fact, sometimes they are! They may not even be religious, yet they have some capacity within to think and perceive beyond this world, beyond the concrete existence.

For example, some people never think about what is going to happen to them after death. For others, life after death is a normal and natural part of their faith in God. Some people do not believe in angels and demons; others view this world as a virtual battleground with spiritual warfare going on invisibly all around us that only those who are clued in can see. Some people are "tuned in" to the mystical aspects of life; others are "tuned out."

Most of the major religions of the world acknowledge that God is a spirit. God is not a human being, so if you want to know him, you must worship him in spirit and truth. Yet many people in our world don't agree with this because they are sensually oriented rather than spiritually oriented. They have to see it, feel it, touch it, taste it, or hear it before they will believe.

Obviously, if two people are on different wavelengths when it comes to issues of spirituality, one or both of them are going to think the other is a little off his or her rocker! Those people who are not spiritual have difficulty in understanding those who are spiritually inclined. Individuals for whom spirituality comes naturally cannot understand how other people can be so cavalier and calloused that they cannot perceive spiritual things. Obviously, people who have similar spiritual perspectives will do much better together.

Getting extremely practical in the area of spirituality, two partners in marriage will have the most satisfaction when they share the most agreement in their faith. That's why I believe it is best for Christians to marry Christians, Jewish people to marry Jewish people, Muslims to marry Muslims, and so on. Mixing religious faiths does not make each stronger; it dilutes both. This is not isolationism; it is simply good psychology. Moreover, within Christianity I am convinced that partners will usually fare better if they marry within their general denominations—Catholics with Catholics, Protestants with Protestants. Those who think such matters are irrelevant fail to comprehend that religion, while being one of the greatest unifying forces on earth, can also be one of the most divisive. If you have any doubt about that, follow the news on any given day, and you will notice that most of the major problems between people in the world today can be traced to religious origins.

On a personal level, I always know a couple are headed for trouble when one person wants to get greatly involved in the church, attend Bible studies and prayer sessions, give a minimum of 10 percent of his or her income to the church, while the other person has no interest in such matters. Don't even think about minimizing spiritual issues. Surprisingly, spiritual matters become even more focused after the wedding day, and especially when the children start coming along. Some individuals and couples who never before felt greatly inclined to pursue a relationship with God suddenly don't want to live without him. That doesn't always sit well with a partner who is not well matched with you in the area of spirituality.

Madeline and Randy are a case in point. Randy said, "Madeline never mentioned going to church before we were married. But a few months after our wedding, she started to get real religious. She didn't want to party anymore. She quit drinking alcoholic beverages and became insistent that I do the same. I said, 'Hey babe, if you don't want to drink, that's up to you. But don't push your religion onto me.'

"When we started having kids, she really flipped out. Suddenly it was important to take the kids to church all the time. This religion thing has really divided us. I feel as if I'm being left out of my own family."

Maybe Madeline did not realize spiritual matters would become so important to her, but she, like many others, quickly discovered that marriage, family, and spiritual life belong together. That's why I strongly urge you to talk through your spiritual similarities and differences, preferably before you get involved in a serious relationship and definitely before you get married. To have a successful marriage, it is important that you and your mate are similar in your beliefs about the role of religion in your lives. If you find yourself diverging to any great extent, you must step back and reconsider your relationship. Two totally irreligious people have a better chance of faring well in marriage than a couple divided by spiritual matters.

Sherry loved to attend enthusiastic church services, but she was married to a man who rarely went to church with her. When he did go, he sat in the back of the sanctuary and couldn't wait to get out of the building following the final "amen." Not surprisingly, their marriage fell apart. They were on different wavelengths on a crucial matching dimension.

Sherry remained single for nine years, dating a few men but never developing a quality relationship with anyone. When she met Doug, however, she knew immediately that something was different. Doug enjoyed going to church, with Sherry or without her. When they attended services together, Sherry was impressed at Doug's willingness to sing the congregational hymns and choruses robustly. When he prayed, Doug talked to God as though he truly believed God could hear him and would answer. As she and Doug sat in the congregation listening to the sermons and other teachings, Sherry felt closer to Doug than any man she had ever known. They were not simply physically attracted; they were drawn together spiritually. Their marriage was truly a match made in heaven! And that's a good spiritual match!

CHAPTER 13

DIMENSION **11** | Education

THE CORE DIMENSION of education may be considered more mal-leable than others. You can go back to school or take correspondence courses online to get more education even if you are retirement age. But it is still wise to count the costs. The fact is: As much as they may desire to do so, most people do not go back to school once they are out of their thirties. In that case, we'd be more realistic to look at where you are today when trying to find your soul mate, rather than where you want to be when you complete the next phase of your self-help program.

Years ago, I could build a strong case that as long as individuals were similar in their intelligence levels, their actual formal education would not make a big difference to them. Over the years, as I've confronted the clinical evidence of couples in my office on the brink of calling it quits, I've had to change my thinking on this dimension. I am now convinced that having similar educational backgrounds does indeed matter. If you are not closely matched in your levels of education, at the very minimum you should have a similar apprecia-tion for the value of education and the hard work that it requires.

This dimension is particularly sensitive to women, especially women who have completed college or graduate school. Usually edu-cated women need to be matched with men who have equal or better levels of education. For instance, we have some female circuit court judges with several law degrees, high intelligence, and six-figure in-comes on eHarmony; they are not going to match well with somebody who has only a high school education.

While it cannot be denied that many marriages work well despite educational inequality, the issue of having a degree becomes more important if your family places a lot of emphasis on "getting your education." If that is your history, you should definitely avoid dating relationships with people of the opposite sex who do not have a good bit of formal education or at least a great appreciation for it, and who would find that part of your personality valuable, attractive, and appealing.

A good friend of mine married into a family in which almost everybody has a PhD degree. Obviously, in that family, education matters, and although some may cringe at this thought, a certain "here's looking down at you" attitude would surely have greeted any-one marrying into the family without a formal education.

On the other hand, Aaron was the first member of his family to ever go to college. He went on to earn his master's degree before he met Amber, who had graduated from high school and gone straight into an office job, where she worked her way up the corporate ladder to a supervisor's position. To Aaron, Amber's lack of formal educa-tion didn't seem to matter as much, because she had accomplished a degree of success in her field. Nevertheless, he sometimes became frustrated when she couldn't relate to a classic book or play he re-ferred to in casual conversation. Great art and literature eluded her as well, and as much as Aaron attempted to expose Amber to cultural aspects of life that he had come to expect as normal, Amber simply wasn't on the same page with him.

A longtime family friend named Carol never received anything lower than an A in any course in high school. She was extremely bright and was offered a full tuition scholarship to an important midwestern university. That was a big deal for a young girl living in the middle of America!

But her dad said to her, "Why would you want to do that? Why don't you go to work and make some money?"

Essentially, her dad was implying (in a day when such implica-tions were the norm) that girls didn't need to go to college. After all, aren't you simply going to settle down, get married, and have babies? That was her very traditional dad, and in those days, traditional young women didn't buck the wishes of their dads.

Although Carol did not attend college, she was attracted to bright men nonetheless, and she married a man with a PhD. They have remained married for more than sixty years!

Recently Carol and I were discussing this matter when I broached a delicate part of the subject. "Carol, what has that been like for your marriage partner to have so much education and you to have so little? I've always felt that the difference in education was never a big thing for you two, because you have a high level of intellect in common. Is that right, or has it ever been a problem?"

Carol looked back at me incredulously. "Neil, it has been horrible!"

"Really? How so?"

"He was always embarrassed that I had not gone to college," Carol replied. "And I always felt awkward when we'd go to parties together, and I'd meet his friends or coworkers. I knew that eventually they were going to ask me where I had gone to school. I was always uncomfortable, feeling that I was right on the edge of being embarrassed. Beyond that, he's often put me down in subtle ways for my lack of formal education; he's hurt my feelings many times. I bear many inner scars from his put-downs. It has been miserable."

That conversation truly shocked me. If ever I had seen a couple that had enough brightness in common to compensate for a lack of similarities in educational backgrounds and overcome any potential intimidation, it was my friend and her husband. Some people may be able to pull it off, but they sure couldn't.

"I used to hate going to my wife's college reunions," Eric confessed. "While she'd be talking with former classmates about the various fun activities that they did on campus, and remembering old professor so-and-so who used to wear two different-colored socks, I'd be over in the corner drinking. I just couldn't relate to all that. I never went to college, had no desire to go to college, and I've made a good living for our family. As a matter of fact, in many ways I've been far more successful in my career than most of those people who are still paying on their college loans. Patty says it doesn't bother her that I never went to college, that we have a better life than most of her college friends. Yet when we get around those people, the glaring differences between us seem to overshadow everything else."

Prejudices about education flow in both directions. "He's so smart that he's stupid," said Emily in explaining why she had broken up with Bruce. "He is absolutely brilliant when it comes to talking about scientific formulas, and he knows how to fix a computer faster than I can even turn it on, but when it comes to common sense, he just can't relate to the rest of the world. I used to have to remind him to put his paychecks in the bank, because he'd just leave them lying around on his desk for weeks while he worked on some new invention out in the garage." It's probably a good thing that Emily and Bruce broke up.

As in most of the twenty-nine dimensions, if you will find someone who is a lot like you, you can avoid some of the hurt and pain that come from being mismatched in the area of education. Again, it is not a question of how much education you or your partner have or don't have; the important issue is how closely you match. Only in rare instances have I ever met a happily married couple who had wide differences in this area. While it is impossible to attach grade levels or degrees to marital happiness, it seems that couples who are closer in academic achievements are better matched in other areas as well.

CHAPTER 14

DIMENSION **12** | Appearance

IF THERE IS any dimension in which most people feel competent to select their own potential marriage partners, it is in the area of appearance. Ask most men or women what type of look they like in the opposite sex, and few will have difficulty in telling you. (Although many of our images and expectations about what we like have been greatly distorted by movies and magazines.)

Everyone wants to be matched with someone who is attractive, but how attractive? What level of attractiveness is reasonable for you to desire in a potential partner? While the nerdy-looking guy and the fashion model make for comedic movies and contrived romance novels, that usually doesn't happen in real life. If you are an average-looking person who aspires to marry someone who looks as though they just stepped out of a fashion magazine, you will probably be disappointed. Super-attractive people usually marry other super-attractive people. We "commoners" do better with fellow commoners. Are there exceptions? Oh, my, yes! Does that make for a good relationship? Sometimes, but not often.

Most men and women are much more comfortable being matched with someone in a range of attractiveness similar to their own. Imagine a seven-point scale of personal attractiveness, with one being less attractive and seven being the most attractive person. Men usually rate themselves a bit higher than an objective group of their peers might rate them; women, however, tend to rate themselves lower on an appearance scale. Even fashion models often have a diminished view of their own appearance.

Beyond that, only about 5 percent of the men and women in the entire population are thought to be handsome or beautiful by an objective jury of observers. In other words, most of us won't ever be on the annual year end's "Most Beautiful People" lists. Consequently, about 95 percent of the population are chasing the other 5 percent. Good luck! How can you compete with that?

Here's one idea: Our culture has accepted certain "looks" that some people esteem as attractive. For example, some women really like a "tall, dark, and handsome" man. Some men prefer perky, blue-eyed blondes. In searching for a mate, you should migrate toward people who appreciate your type of appearance, the same features that other people may not appreciate as much. If you come from a family where the valued standard of beauty is dark hair and skin, you are more likely to find acceptance in groups that look a lot like your relatives. They might rate you higher on appearance simply because they value that particular look.

Despite society's recent emphasis on the sleek, slender, svelte figure, some people prefer a partner who has a more stocky, sturdy, or muscular build. These variables are all a matter of taste when it comes to appearance.

I do know, however, from my extensive clinical research that men who are "fives" on our seven-point scale do better in a relationship when they are matched with women who are fives or sixes. Similarly, when women are matched with someone on their same level or above, they seem to do well. Too much disparity causes concern, although something amazing happens when people fall in love. Suddenly, they will typically rate their partners one or two points higher than an objective group of their peers might rate those same persons. In addition, when individuals get to know each other on eHarmony before they see each other face-to-face, they tend to rate each other's appearance higher. I'm convinced that when you fall in love for all the right reasons, when you fall in love with the *person* rather than his or her appearance, even someone of less physical attractiveness becomes more desirable to you.

It is much easier to deal with appearance after you have gotten to know the inner qualities of a person than it is to deal with the inner person after you have become habituated to a person's appearance.

Once you are hooked on that person's appearance, you are tempted to overlook important deficiencies and sometimes glaring inconsistencies in his or her life. Because you became enamored with "the wrappings," you are more prone to miss the true person inside. Sadly, that is one of the major causes of marriage failures today. When the wrappings come off and the true person is revealed, it is often not a pretty sight if the other twenty-eight dimensions are not well matched. With the transient qualities of beauty nowadays, it makes even more good sense to fall in love from the inside out.

What about cosmetic surgery? Will a face-lift, nose job, breast enhancement or reduction, liposuction, Botox treatments to cover frown lines and wrinkles, or a raft of other surgical procedures make a new man or woman out of you? What about a crash-course weight-loss program or some other appearance-altering regimen? Can't that change the way a person looks, thus making him or her more aesthetically pleasing? Of course; and for a person for whom cosmetic surgery or physical fitness programs are safe, that may be a helpful way to boost that person's self-conception, which will result in his or her becoming more attractive to the opposite sex. Tragically, though, with the modern proliferation and accessibility of cosmetic surgery, many people are traipsing from doctor to doctor hoping to improve their external body parts, when the real transformation that will make them more attractive to others must take place on the inside.

Moreover, appearance tends to become less important in a relationship as the years pass. But character issues and traits such as kindness and compassion will still be important, and will usually go up in value over the years.

Beyond that, we all are in a losing battle with age. The secret to contentment is to be happy with your body at whatever age you happen to be. Do the best you can to care for your appearance, but if you concentrate on the inner person, you will be more likely to find your soul mate. What is more beautiful than two elderly grandparents whose skin may be a bit wrinkled, but the sparkle in their eyes for each other is undiminished?

CHAPTER 15

DIMENSION **13** | Sense of Humor

A GOOD SENSE OF HUMOR shows up on virtually every "mate shopping list" I've ever seen. In fact, a mutual ability to laugh is always in the top five on everybody's lists. Beyond the fact that a good sense of humor is an extremely attractive quality to most people (someone has said, "Smile; it will increase your face-value!"), humor contributes a wealth of highly therapeutic elements to a marriage. The old saying "Laughter is good medicine" is really true, especially when a marriage is going through tough times, a period of stress, calamity, or struggle. Marriages in which there is little laughter tend to do worse during the good times and *much worse* during the bad times.

"He cracks me up all the time," Christina said of her boyfriend, Jared. "He doesn't even try to be funny; he just is. He makes me smile . . . but I worry that I hardly ever make him laugh."

Because we all desire a good sense of humor in a mate, we tend to think that we have to try to be funny during a date or when we initially meet people. That can be a little intimidating for a person who is not inclined to tell jokes, fire off wisecracks, or let fly quick quips from the hip.

But I have good news! You don't need to be able to *generate* humor to have a good marriage. Nor is it important that you have the same ability to be witty as your partner. You just need to be able to *appreciate* humor.

Our daughter Luann is an extremely bright young woman with a PhD in psychology. Luann's interpersonal charm is not because she's so witty, but because she has a marvelous gift for appreciating humor.

She is a great laugher! Just hearing Luann laugh is enough to lift your spirits even on the most stressful of days.

I recall when young high school boys used to come to our home to work with her on a school assignment, and it would always intrigue me to listen to them interacting. The boys would rattle off story after story, and Luann would respond with uninhibited laughter. The boys would break out in uproarious laughter themselves. The boys would then talk some more, and Luann would laugh some more! I mean, she just had the best time laughing during their conversations. Not surprisingly, Luann was an extremely popular girl in her high school. People enjoy being around someone who knows how to laugh. Luann didn't tell jokes or funny stories; she just had an ability to appreciate humor, and the guys loved that! Usually, most women love that trait in men as well.

What could be worse than to be in a relationship with someone who is always dour? You say something funny, and he or she just sits there with a stone-faced expression. Who wants to live with *that*?

I'm convinced that a highly developed sense of humor, and the ability to laugh at the same places in life, relates deeply to a shared perspective on life events. What we find funny, and what we don't, probably reflects several of the twenty-nine dimensions that make up a good relationship. For example, when you and your partner both laugh at the same things, it may indicate that you have similar values; it may reflect that you have similar intelligence and the same ability to take in and process information. Humor often involves some punch line or twist that actually makes it funny, and when you both "get it," that probably says something about your similar interests and intelligence levels. On the other hand, if one person gets it but the other does not, be careful. If a person has a tendency to not get a joke, what does that say about his or her outlook on life, educational background, family background, or overall general attitude?

Likewise, if the person in whom you are interested is constantly laughing at his or her own jokes, it may reflect problems in the areas of self-conception, nervousness, and discomfort within himself or herself.

Certainly, *what* we laugh at says something about a person's character. If your partner's or your own humor centers around meanness or other people's misfortune, mistakes, or inabilities, watch out. Such humor can become a two-edged sword, cutting both ways. If somebody has a sense of humor that is riddled with sarcasm, sprinkled with cutting remarks that can verbally chop a person off at the knees in one swipe, be very careful. While that humor may be extremely funny before you are married, after you are married you can be sure that same sarcasm will be aimed at you, and it won't feel so funny.

Terry is a bombastic, boisterous fellow naturally, and when he combines his quick-thinking personality with razor-sharp sarcasm, he can be downright dangerous. Before he and Vickie were married, Terry often joked about his former girlfriends, making snide remarks about everything from their weight to their breath. Vickie couldn't keep from laughing aloud at Terry's shredding of one of her rivals. Unfortunately, it wasn't long after they were married that Vickie realized the viciousness of her husband's humor as he turned the blade of sarcasm on her.

Listen carefully to what you laugh about in your relationship. For example, some people relish a humor that is steeped in racism. Yet at the base of racism is usually hatred, fear, suspicion, mean-spiritedness, or other forms of an aggressive approach to differences. It is an indication of a lack of good self-conception. Inevitably, the person who laughs the hardest at racist humor doesn't feel very good about himself or herself.

The same is true of inappropriate sexual humor. Much of our humor nowadays has subtle sexual overtones, but blatant sexual humor almost always reflects a person who is disturbed within some area of his or her sexuality. Any humor that makes fun of the agony that people experience in their sexuality is usually an indication of past hurt or unresolved conflict and pain in the jokester's life. He or she may be funny when you are dating or when you are with a group at a party, but that same person may be mean, moody, and morose at home. If a person's humor has a slicing edge to it, you would be wise to beware. Humor that is about somebody else's pain will ultimately bring a relationship into a less healthy place.

CHAPTER 16

DIMENSION **14** | Mood Management

A FEW YEARS AGO we had an employee at eHarmony who was a loner, and for good reason. A passive-aggressive personality, he simply exuded a "keep away from me" attitude, almost like a skunk giving off a foul scent that warns everyone to flee.

One day I stopped at the doorway of the fellow's office and asked, "Is Jake in yet this afternoon?"

"No, he's gone," the fellow replied, hardly looking up from his desk. We had recently remodeled, and I hadn't yet seen the new office, so I popped my head inside to look around. When I did, he looked up and said, "What do you think, that he's hiding in there?"

His words stung. Besides the fact that I am the founder of the company and have the right to inspect whatever I want, his tone of disrespect would have been inappropriate for any visitor in the office.

I glared at him and said intently, "When you come at me that way, you really make me mad."

"Oh, hey, I was just joking," he said, trying to cover his mistake now that he knew I was upset. "I was just trying to be funny."

I went home that night and didn't sleep well. Nor did I sleep well the following night. It wasn't that the fellow didn't deserve to be rebuked; he did. But what I had missed was his pain. He is passive-aggressive, all doubled over inside himself in an effort to be vengeful, but mostly to keep people from getting close to him.

I had missed that, and I didn't want to further his problem. I didn't want to make him feel even more unsafe and cause him to send out an even worse aroma to others. I should have said something like, "I'm not quite sure why you said that, but it stung me. And it kind of hurt me. Did you really think that I was doubting your word?"

Dealing with somebody who suffers from extreme mood fluctuations is tricky business. If you or your partner has big fluctuations in moods, you need to be able to handle that or at least be tolerant of it.

Some mood changes are the result of diet. When a person doesn't eat, he or she gets snippy. A perfectly happy-go-lucky person turns into Attila the Hun around four o'clock every afternoon because his or her body is crying out for food. A piece of fruit, a granola bar, or some other quick-energy snack may save you from a divorce if you are married to a person who suffers from severe mood swings. Similarly, when people get extremely stressed or fatigued, they can become unusually irritable. This sort of provocative mood swing is often beyond the normal run-down feeling that a person may feel after a good day's work or activity.

"I can't tell what is a major crisis in our relationship or what is simply an ordinary frustration of everyday life," lamented Dennis. "Marsha responds pretty much the same way to a flat tire as she does to a death in the family! She'll call me on my cell phone just bawling, and I'm worried that something catastrophic has happened when, in fact, she's merely gotten a spot on her new carpet."

If that couple get married, Dennis is going to need an extra dose of tolerance and patience, but Marsha needs to get some specific medical or psychological help to get to the bottom of the reason for her emotional outbursts. Such major mood fluctuations most often have to do with some chemical deficiency in a person's body. Regardless, their marriage is going to have to carry that extra burden, and after a while, if they don't get help, it will be all too easy to slump into depression and despair.

If mood fluctuations are frequent and extreme, be very careful about entering a long-term relationship with that person. It is critical that a couple be aware of any such fluctuations before getting married. If you are the person whose moods vacillate so dramatically, you owe it to your partner to inform him or her (although it's quite likely they have already noticed). It's a little tougher to gather such information if it is your partner who suffers from such severe fluctuations. Before you are married, you may not see the person at his or her lowest points. That's another good reason for giving your relationship plenty of time to see each other in the best of circumstances and in the worst. But even with plenty of time, you must be bold enough to discuss such matters. It's too late once you are married. You don't want to wake up next to someone for the rest of your life who may be ready one day to kiss you passionately and the next day to bite your head off. Consistency is the key to a good match in the area of mood management.

CHAPTER 17

DIMENSION **15** | Traditional Versus Nontraditional Personalities

The first time Terry heard the lyrics to "Are You Going to San Francisco?" he made up his mind that's where he wanted to be—where all the girls wore flowers in their hair, and everyone under thirty years of age hung out on the street corners of Haight-Ashbury—when they weren't smoking pot or experimenting with hallucinogenic drugs such as LSD. It was the late 1960s and like many disgruntled collegians, Terry was afraid of being drafted into the war in Vietnam. He wasn't so much of a passionate antiwar zealot as he was simply fearful. But the hippie movement of the 1960s and early 1970s popularized the idea of dropping out of the establishment, mainstream society, and dropping in wherever one pleased.

It pleased Terry to drop in at a crowded San Francisco apartment where six or eight other drifters slept on a dirty mattress in a haze-filled back room, with strung beads serving as doors. A fair to decent guitar player and songwriter, Terry whiled away the next three or four years—he was never quite sure how long he was there—composing his own music and singing in coffeehouses. He also wrote numerous antiwar tracts and other diatribes that were published in the local papers under various names. In the process, Terry became rather adept at writing searing articles that piqued the interest and pricked the consciences of those who bothered to read them.

Sometime in the early 1970s, Terry met Katherine—he called her Kate—the daughter of an upper-middle-class couple from the suburbs outside Chicago. They fell in love and had a barefoot wedding under a lightpole on a cool summer evening. Most of the "invited guests" never remembered being there, but Terry and Kate took their vows seriously. They eventually quit doing drugs and moved back to New York where, thanks to Kate's father's connections, she was able to get an entry-level job working at a stockbrokerage. Terry started an "alternative underground newspaper" in which he expressed his opinions about everything from politics to religion to reviews of off-Broadway shows.

Slowly but surely, Kate began to rise in the company's ranks. She bought some stylish new clothes, reclaimed her name, and once again began referring to herself as Katherine. Meanwhile, Terry continued to function pretty much as he had in San Francisco, minus the drugs. He was a free spirit who refused to plan for the future, even for the next week. Increasingly, his lack of goals, motivation, or any desire to get ahead in life irritated Katherine. She was receiving one promotion after another at the brokerage and had plans to be a broker herself within a year or two. She began dressing in designer clothes, while Terry continued to wear his flannel shirts, refusing to become "a part of the problem." The chasm between them widened as, more and more, Katherine realized that she really wanted a lifestyle much like that of her parents', including a white-collar, traditional crowd of friends who actually worked for a living and golfed at the club on weekends.

The divorce was relatively simple, especially since Terry and Katherine never knew whether they were legally married or not, but it was not without a great deal of pain and animosity. Even in the most idealistic of worlds, reality still says that the hippie and the stockbroker just aren't a good match. They are simply too different in their approaches to life.

Terry and Katherine's story leads us to another core dimension, the overall traditional personality orientation versus the nontraditional personality orientation, and reminds us of a profound point: If two individuals are highly nontraditional in their personalities and approaches to life, as were Kate and Terry in San Francisco, they can get along quite well. But if one person is traditional and another has a bit of an eccentric streak, or purposely chooses to buck the accepted traditions, you can count on trouble in that relationship.

Traditional Versus Nontraditional Personalities

If one person likes life to be rather predictable and prefers to plan for events such as birthday parties, vacations, or weddings, you are probably dealing with a traditional type of personality. On the other hand, if you or your partner loves to just "go with the flow," doing what comes naturally or whatever happens to inspire at the moment, you should expect a lot of spontaneity and nontraditional personality quirks. The problem, of course, is that when a planner and a free spirit get together; you will usually end up with friction leading to spontaneous combustion.

Sometimes nontraditional people have grown up with frustration and anger in relation to the pressures of societal customs. Their anger may be buried deeply within or expressed in more acceptable ways— protesting a controversial war, in Terry's case; promoting flagrantly antitraditional lifestyles, as can be seen in many activist groups today. They are basically saying, "I've been hurt and I'm mad, and I am not going to conform to you or anyone else!" Many nontraditional people continue to carry that social anger with them long after the fact. They do not wish to give traditional society any credit for maintaining the very order that allows for nonconformity, because in their view, traditional society has hurt their feelings so much. We saw this attitude manifested in many ways through the music, movies, and television programs produced in the late 1960s and the 1970s. And, of course, we see a similar trend today.

Other nontraditional types simply enjoy the freedom to be different. They don't want to be encumbered by the constraints of "normal" society. They regard traditionalists to be boring; they'd much rather be risk-takers. That's fine, but if you are more of a traditionalist and try to maintain a relationship with a nontraditional person, it can keep you feeling disorganized and disconcerted.

"Cody just drives me so crazy that sometimes I think I'm going to explode!" Norita said as she exhaled in exasperation. "He refuses to give me a time frame in which he thinks we might be able to get married, and he won't even sit still long enough to talk about it. He says it will all come together at the proper time."

From Cody's standpoint, he knows he is not yet ready for marriage, so he regards Norita's incessant prodding to set a date for their wedding as being obsessive. "Is that all you ever think about?" he asked jokingly.

"Yes!" Norita nearly shouted.

Certainly, the traditional versus nontraditional approaches to life can grate against you if your partner and you are dissimilar. Norita wants to start saving money for their wedding; she spends weekends looking into apartments or affordable starter homes, and she has already begun exploring the job possibilities that might provide basic health-care benefits. Norita is a planner. She hates surprises.

Cody, on the other hand, is a spontaneous personality who thinks nothing of throwing some clothes in a duffel bag and heading off on a weeklong trip across the country, with hardly enough money to buy food.

Are these two people good marriage material? Only if they have strong matches in twenty-eight other areas, because their life together will be one of constant tension or compromise on this dimension. The real question they each must ask is, "Can I live with that?" Or, perhaps a stronger query: "Do I want to willfully place myself in a position where I *must* live with that?"

What complicates matters more is that people with opposite personality traits often find each other extremely attractive. Mark Twain observed that there are two kinds of people in this world: one who is always ten minutes early, and another who is always ten minutes late. Furthermore, Twain added sardonically, "They're always married to each other!"

As we noted earlier, opposites do attract. They click as a couple for a while because they complement each other, perhaps subconsciously finding their "completion" in the other person. After a while, they say, "Hey, this is really working! Let's get married." The quiet, subdued, passive person then marries the loud, dynamic, controlling person; the spontaneous, irresponsible person marries a more stable and conservative type; the "neatnik" marries the slovenly. Then each person proceeds to pursue the prime purpose of marriage (in their minds at least): attempting to change his or her partner into a reproduction of himself or herself.

What concerns me when two people are at odds in the traditional versus nontraditional dimension is that they often become habituated. For example, some nontraditional people grow accustomed to dressing in a sloppy manner, because that's what their peer group accepts. Their appearance becomes part of their persona. In many cases, their nonconformity eventually becomes the norm. (Are they then conforming to nonconformity? It gets confusing!) But that is not what the rest of society finds attractive, acceptable, or indicative of a person of quality and character. Certainly, many of these stigmas are cultural and will change from group to group, from one generation to the next. But that doesn't mean they don't exist.

When that nontraditional person then goes out to find a job, he suddenly discovers that while creativity is welcomed, nonconformity is not. A college student, for example, who spent four years or more developing his or her nonconformity wearing frumpy clothes and railing about the inequities of the world, now must put on a suit if he or she wishes to compete in the current corporate business culture.

Our corporate culture at eHarmony is rather laid-back, but it is definitely not sloppy. When Grant Langston, one of our first employees, came to work with us, it was a shock to his system. If Grant ever came in to work wearing a suit, we'd think he was applying for a job somewhere else! Suits simply weren't (and still aren't) Grant's style. But little by little, I noticed that Grant was upgrading his wardrobe. By his own admission, he has no desire to be a fashion plate, but passing through our building today, his clothing usually doesn't cause anyone to raise an eyebrow.

Early on, when Grant was coming to grips with the statement his appearance was making, he quipped, "Do you think I would want to work for any business that would want somebody who looks like I do today?" We laughed with him then, and today we are proud and appreciative of the manner in which Grant represents our company.

In a similar way, you must ask yourself that sort of question if you are involved with a person who leans toward being a nontraditional-ist. Obviously, many nontraditional types can be extremely creative, but if you are a more traditional type of person, you would be wise to take a realistic look at that and say, "Yes, those quirks are interesting, but will those same quirks eventually drive me crazy? Do I really want to live with that?"

Maybe you do . . . or maybe you don't, but you must make that assessment before moving into marriage.

CHAPTER 18

DIMENSION **16** | Ambition

IT MAY SURPRISE YOU to see "ambition" among those core characteristics that are relatively difficult to change, but if you've ever tried to motivate a person with low ambition, you probably understand well. Once again, however, matching well in this area is not primarily a matter of how much ambition you and your partner have; the important issue is that you have similar amounts of ambition.

A highly motivated, competitive, zealous, "get-up-get-moving-get-ahead" type of person is simply not going to enjoy being married to a person who is content with the status quo and merely wants to "kick back and enjoy life." If there is a great discrepancy between the amount of ambition the two partners possess, inevitably there will be stress and increased conflict in that relationship. One person passionately wants to pursue his or her goals, while the other person resents the time, effort, money, and energy expended to do so.

All Karen ever wanted was a good, honest husband who would love her, treat her with kindness, and stay home with her and the kids she hoped to have. Curtis, the man she is dating, is a warm, generous, upstanding man who is deeply committed to his career, working with a children's home. The sheer amount of time and energy he pours into serving the children takes him away from Karen more than she is comfortable in handling. "I feel that my greatest ambition is to be a wife and a mother," said Karen with tears dotting her cheeks, "and that doesn't seem to be enough for Curtis. He spends long hours at the children's home, and I certainly don't begrudge him for that. But if we are ever going to have a home and a family ourselves, I don't know that I can live with his being gone so much of the time."

Problems due to differences in ambition levels will surface most often within the first five to ten years of marriage. Unquestionably, this is why so many people on a fast track in their careers have trouble holding their marriages together. Men and women who pour themselves into their careers—some because the career demands it, others because they are simply so passionate about it—have little left to give to their spouses at a time when the spouses really need them. No wonder we see professional athletes, politicians, medical doctors, and other high-pressure occupations churning out so many divorces.

Many medical doctors, for example, must work twenty-four-hour shifts when they become residents. During the early part of his career, that doctor's spouse better be equally as committed to their success, or the marriage will suffer irreparable harm.

On the other hand, when you have two people who are on similar tracks regarding ambition, they can be tremendous encouragers to each other. Marylyn is a hard worker. She gets up early and starts working immediately. She will work long into the night if necessary to accomplish her goals. Consequently, she motivates me and liberates me to give free rein to my more ambitious dreams. One of my goals, as I mentioned previously, is to help reduce the divorce rate in America by 1 percent each year. That is my primary motivation for getting up and going to work each morning when we could have already retired or planted ourselves on some tropical beach for the rest of our lives. As much as we enjoy rest and relaxation—and force ourselves to take a break from time to time—Marylyn and I are ambitious by nature. There's more to be done; more to explore, more possibilities and opportunities, whole vistas we have yet to explore.

And I am an extremely blessed man to have a mate who is as ambitious as I am. Can you imagine how frustrating that would be for both of us if Marylyn was not interested in eHarmony, or if she wasn't willing to back our commitment with a commensurate level of hard work, or at least a tolerance of my giving so much of myself to our business? We would be *miserable*! Sadly, many couples are unhappy because they do not match well in the area of ambition.

Understand, when considering ambition, we are not merely talking about making money or making a mark on the world through a career. You can be extremely altruistic and be very ambitious at the same time. You may be ambitious about changing the fabric of society; you may work indefatigably for your favorite political party; you may pour yourself into alleviating hunger, or helping to take care of the millions of people in Africa afflicted with AIDS. But if you are in a relationship with someone who does not share your ambition, it is going to be a tough road for one or both of you.

On the other hand, if you find someone with whom you can share a similar level of ambition, your life together can be one of contentment, even when you are working in some frenetic way to accomplish a task, beat a deadline, or meet a need. Of course, if you both have a low level of ambition and are content to just make ends meet, live in relative obscurity, and simply enjoy being together, that's fine, too. Just make sure that you both match in regard to ambition. Otherwise, your relationship is likely to suffer, especially in the area of sexual passion and intimacy.

Let's look at that next!

CHAPTER 19

DIMENSION **17** | Sexual Passion

IN THE MOVIE *Annie Hall*, the characters played by Woody Allen and Diane Keaton are shown simultaneously lamenting about their sex lives to their therapists. She complains, "He wants sex all the time. At least four times a week." On a split screen, he tells the doctor they almost never have sex: "Four times a week at most."

Clearly, the dimension of sexual passion is a matter of perspective, but it is one in which partners who want a good relationship must be rather closely matched. It simply makes good sense that in this most intimate of human interaction, a man and a woman ought to have similar attitudes, interests, and desires.

If a man has a great deal of testosterone and his wife has low sexual desire, that is a formula for trouble. The man will feel rejected and unsatisfied, and the woman will feel badgered, manipulated, and used every time he pushes her for more sexual intimacy. Obviously, this is not going to be a fun couple!

Interestingly, a great dilemma in our society today is that we have noncommunicative men who are highly sexualized trying to match with highly communicative, less sexualized women. A woman wants to know what a man is thinking, what he is feeling; she wants him to care about her and to be interested in what *she* is thinking and feeling before she ever considers sharing her body with him. Men think, *Let's just have sex, then we'll talk . . . if we absolutely must*. It is almost a perennial complaint that marriage therapists hear—that one partner is more sexually inclined than the other.

While it is possible that two people who have extremely low interest in sex could be compatible, it is certainly preferable to want a high level of sexual passion in your relationship. In fact, I often tell single women that the last thing you want is a man who has an extremely low level of sexual passion. If you've been with the same man for a while, and he never pressures you for sex and never wants to "take you out to the woods" (my favorite euphemism for engaging in intimate sexual expressions), and if he never wants to play his radio in the car with the headlights off and no moon in the sky, and if he never really puts the pressure on you to make an important boundary decision in the area of sex, *be careful of that man*!

After dating Michael for several months, Brittany went home and told her mother, "You know, Mom; Michael is such a gentleman. He never seems to be all that sex crazed, like some of the other guys I've dated. We've been dating now for several months, and he's never laid a hand on me; he's never even tried to kiss me." As much as her mom appreciated Michael's morality or modesty, Brittany had every reason to wonder about his level of sexual passion. But she let the matter slide and a few months later, she and Michael had a lovely wedding. A few days into the honeymoon, Brittany returned home. She and Michael still had not consummated their relationship. She had married a man who no doubt will drive her bonkers over time because of his lack of interest in sexual activity. You want a marriage partner who is highly sexualized.

The second thing I tell single women is: If you want to make a determination about how you will do sexually with a man, kiss him. The kiss is the best diagnostic device known to mankind for determining how your and your mate's levels of sexual excitement will compare. If imaginary flames fly all around you when your lips touch, then you know you probably have plenty of passion there, and most sexuality will be good if there is plenty of passion. You don't want to marry someone who has a lot less or a lot more sexual passion than you do. You want to marry someone with similar values and attitudes about sex and similar physical desires.

Obviously, the focus of this book is not about sex. Our main concern here is that you understand how important it is that you and your partner are well matched in the area of sexuality. At eHarmony, we assess your level of sexual passion based on your responses to the

questions we ask in your personality profile, and we take that information into consideration in matching you with someone with similar sexual passion. But it is one of the most difficult and delicate parts
of our matching process.

Part of the difficulty stems from the fact that in every other dimension, we encourage you to fully explore your partner as best you can,
to delve into his or her family background, to consider carefully how
closely you match in intelligence, to gather as much information as
possible about your partner's ambition and all the other essential dimensions. While we do the same in the area of sexual passion, we
recognize how crucial it is to maintain your objectivity at every step
of the process.

A key feature of our position is that early sexual bonding reduces
objectivity. If you are serious about discovering whether you and
your potential partner will match on the twenty-nine dimensions
that make a great relationship, it is crucial that you regulate sexual involvement to maximize your objective analysis and good judgment
at every stage.

The odd dichotomy we face is encouraging people to make sure
they are sexually compatible with a potential marriage partner without encouraging them to be sexually involved with that person. That
raises two obvious questions: Why would we want to do that? And
how is that possible nowadays? Let me answer both questions by
providing you with five broad principles to guide your thoughts
about what sex can be in a great marriage relationship and why you
don't want to squander away something so precious.

1. *Sexual passion is a crucial ingredient between two people if they are to
maintain a long and satisfying relationship.* Some counselors today
want to play down the importance of sex in marriage. I believe that is
a mistake. Granted, sexual passion is only one dimension of a great
relationship, but it is an important one. Moreover, it is one that
should remain; romantic, passionate expressions of love should permeate your marriage all the days of your lives. True, most couples experience a decrease in the frequency of sexual relations after the
initial burst of sexual activity in the early years of their marriage. As

a couple settle into their relationship, they feel more secure, less frenzied, and are thus able to establish a more comfortable, although sometimes less frequent, sexual schedule.

Beyond that, marriage tends to make sex more routine; the day-to-day intimate contact and accessibility sometimes tarnish the sexual luster in a relationship. Nitty-gritty responsibilities of marriage also take a toll. Dealing with mundane household chores and paying monthly bills are not nearly as exciting as the dinner and walk along a moonlit beach you enjoyed before you were married. That is quite normal. But a complete drop-off in sexual passion, or a lack of desire as in the case of Michael, is extremely abnormal.

Many couples make the mistake of allowing the physical aspect of their relationship to take over prior to marriage; consequently, they base many of their decisions on misleading emotions. They may even proceed to marriage based on a satisfying sexual experience, but with insufficient regard to the other twenty-eight dimensions of their relationship. Do I need to tell you what usually happens to those couples within a few years of the wedding?

2. *Sexual passion always involves a strong physical attraction to one another.* These physical expressions are a natural part of your biological and psychological makeup. The desire to touch, to hold each other, to kiss, and other physical expressions flow naturally in a truly loving relationship. To deny that they exist is silly. To give free rein to them before you are married is foolish.

3. *Sexual passion must always be managed with extreme care, but especially before marriage.* Obviously, the safety and comfort of a committed marriage provide the best environment for sexual passion to be expressed, so until that experience is yours, you would be wise to define some strong boundaries to guide your sexual expressions prior to marriage, some lines that you and your partner refuse to cross. It may be too idealistic or naive to think that there will not be a commensurate increase and intensity of physical expressions as a couple move toward a commitment of marriage. But a wise couple will limit these expressions. It will take self-discipline (and sometimes "partner

discipline") to maintain your integrity in view of those limits, but even that is good training for marriage. These boundaries should be discussed between you and your partner "in the cool of the day," when you are both relaxed and comfortable, rather than on the couch at his or her apartment in the wee hours of the morning.

4. *Every expression of sexual passion establishes a new plateau in the relationship.* Once you have moved onto that plateau, it is extremely difficult to back off and be satisfied with less. Many couples start off by holding hands, then progress to hugging, kissing, caressing and fondling through the clothing, skin-to-skin contact, hand-to-genital contact, and eventually genital-to-genital contact. With each increase of contact, the physical aspect takes more control of your relationship. Distinctions get blurred, common sense often goes out the window, and individuals get themselves into trouble because they are making a commitment with their bodies that they are not ready to make with their hearts, minds, and souls. Caught in the throes of sexual passion, many singles get married at a younger age to avoid premarital sexual intercourse, which often creates even more problems, especially if they are not matched in the other twenty-eight vital dimensions.

5. *When sexual passion is not kept in check, you become a slave to your physical desires.* One of the common misconceptions in our world today regarding relationships is: "If we are sexually compatible, that will make everything else about our relationship okay." Nothing could be farther from the truth!

If you "go out to the woods" with a person, it colors every aspect of your relationship; you lose all sense of objectivity in evaluating every other aspect of the relationship. Sex is that powerful. For instance, it is very difficult to be objective about intelligence, obstreperousness, emotional health, or many other components of a good relationship when you are sleeping with a person and engaging in regular sexual intercourse. As I often tell people, sex has a way of short-circuiting your brain.

When you start having orgasms with each other, you flood the neurological pathway so you don't have the ability to think clearly and objectively. This same physiological response occurs in oral sex as well.

After I'd presented a seminar on the subject of relationships at Texas A&M University, a student posed the question: "Dr. Warren, did I understand you correctly? That it is okay if we have intercourse, as long as we don't have orgasm?"

"No, no!" I said. "Intercourse and orgasm are just too intimate to be engaged in outside the total commitment of marriage. They will flood out objectivity and create the potential for you to make numerous serious mistakes regarding your relationship."

If you truly want the best for yourself and your future partner, here are three tips that will help you to keep your sexual expressions before marriage inside the lines. First, write out how you want to be. On a piece of paper or a four-by-five-inch card, write down exactly how you plan to control your sexual passion before marriage and review that card once a day. Memorize it if you can, so you will have an ability to make decisions along the way that will protect you against exploiting yourself physically or exploiting your partner. The key is to make the decision ahead of time, not in the heat of the moment.

My friend Les Parrott was on an airplane flying into a busy airport during a storm. Just as the plane was about to touch down, the pilot made a split-second decision to lift back up. What the passengers didn't know at the time was that another plane was coming in on that same runway from the opposite direction! The pilot pulled the plane up, circled the airport, and made a safe landing. As Les was walking out of the plane, he and the other passengers could see what had nearly happened. Les said to the pilot, "Boy, did you make a good decision! How did you make it so fast?"

The pilot said, "Oh, I made that decision fifteen years ago." In other words, the pilot was saying, "I planned for this moment of crisis long ago. I know what I am going to do in that type of situation before I ever get there."

In the same way, you can plan in advance what you are going to do when the pressures of sexual passion catch you by surprise, and I strongly suggest that you write out what you want to happen, and to plan in advance how you intend to deal with that situation. Like that pilot who had to make a split-second decision in the heat of the moment, make your decision ahead of time.

Second, make sure that you plan your activities and involvements with people of the opposite sex so you don't lose control of the situation. For instance, don't go over to your partner's apartment night after night and merely hang out, or spend long amounts of time in hot and heavy make-out sessions. Sooner or later, if you keep putting your fingers over the fire, you will get burned. Even if you want to make good choices, if you continually subject yourself to intense sexual pressures, you probably won't have the capacity to call off the landing at that point; you will go sailing right through that moment, and you will do whatever comes naturally. Your impulses will have an unbridled opportunity to express themselves.

My friends Joyce and Cliff Penner are professional sex therapists, and Joyce often advises single men and women: "Never make a decision about your sexuality at night. Always plan your decisions about how you are going to handle your sexuality in broad daylight."

That makes sense to me.

Third, find somebody with whom you can talk about sexual matters who is unconditional in their regard for you. In other words, you don't have to worry about offending them, insulting them, or surprising them by your honest questions or by expressing your true feelings, needs, and desires. You can freely tell them exactly where you are in your sexual journey. If you can talk it through with someone who cares for you unconditionally, it will help you get a clearer perspective and help you to unleash all these feelings you have inside.

To sum up, you want to have a lot of sexual passion if you hope to have a good relationship, but you must learn how to put boundaries on it so it doesn't destroy your objectivity, causing you to err in the most important relational decision you will ever make. It is a major issue and, I must caution you, if it is not managed well on this side of marriage, you and your partner are not likely to manage it well once you get married. On the other hand, if you protect this aspect of your relationship until the time when your commitment is total, irrevocable, and permanent, your love, trust, and respect for each other can flourish for a lifetime!

CHAPTER 20

DIMENSION **18** | Artistic Passion

MOST OF US ENJOY the creative arts. We love to hear a great singer or a skilled instrumentalist perform, or to visit an art gallery in which the works of the masters are displayed. We appreciate a beautiful poem or a finely crafted novel.

But while we may appreciate the arts, some people are artistic to the very core of their beings; it is practically in their blood. Sometimes these people may be extremely talented themselves in areas of music, sculpture, writing, painting, photography, drama, or some other creative art. Others cannot perform the art, but they are connoisseurs of the arts; they have a strong interest in observing a performance, watching a powerfully evocative play, or listening to a great piece of music. If you are considering one of these types of artistically inclined individuals as a marriage partner, you'd better be such a person yourself. If a person who has a great deal of artistic passion is matched with someone who does not have the same passion and has little appreciation for it, that relationship is compromised before it even gets started. Most people with strong artistic bents simply must be paired with partners who have similar interests in the arts. If you are an artistic type of person, your partner must match well with you in this area. He or she must not simply be enamored by your ability, success, or acclaim, but must have a genuine appreciation for who you are and what you do.

Mary Beth is a first-chair concert violinist who plays with a well-known symphony in a large American city. When she first met Peter, she was immediately attracted to him and thrilled when he eventually asked her out. During that first date, however, when the discussion turned to music, Peter was quick to rattle off a litany of songs by his favorite hard-rock bands. Unfortunately, he couldn't recall the name of a single piece of classical music, not even Handel's *Messiah*, or Beethoven's Fifth, or the William Tell Overture, or even Mendelssohn's Wedding March.

Sadly—but wisely—Mary Beth refused to go out with Peter again. "We just didn't have a future together," said Mary Beth in explaining to her friends why she broke things off with Peter before they hardly had time to get started. "While we both love music, our tastes are radically different. For Peter, music is entertainment, a nice diversion while he is cleaning out his car. For me, my music is my life."

If you love the violin, don't marry the person who has never heard a violin concerto but loves the Dallas Cowboys. Just imagine saying to him, "After you watch the Cowboys on television today, let's go to the philharmonic."

"The what?" he says.

"The philharmonic."

"What league are they in?"

"Never mind."

For many people who are artistically inclined, their art is central to their lives. It is not merely something they enjoy; it is something they live and breathe. It exudes from their pores. Interestingly, a person with a lot of artistic passion often also has a high level of sexual passion. But if they do not find you present, involved, and appreciative of their artistic passion, the sexual aspect of the relationship will diminish accordingly.

Complicating matters further, many artistic people are also highly nontraditional. Many are loners and nonconformists, and if you think about that, it makes sense. Trace back far enough in the lives of many artistic people, and you will discover that they were not at the center of the social scene among their peers. They usually were not the athletes, and many were not even great students in school. Not necessarily because they weren't intelligent, but because they were disinterested.

Our schools tend to shower a lot of attention on good athletes and kids with good looks. As much as teachers and administrators know better, and most strive to include the quiet, diminutive person-alities in their schools, the natural inclination is to give more notice to those students who are excelling in a popular way. Certainly, prob-lem students receive a lot of attention as well, but that is not the type of person we applaud.

Many more artistic types simply were not the popular kids, and they were sloughed off to the side of social activities during their early schooling. Often, by the time a young man picks up a guitar and starts to sing songs that he has written, it is already late in his ed-ucational process. He may be in his mid- to upper teens before he finds any acceptance and approval for his artistry and, many times, not until much later than that.

A young woman who exhibits talent in painting or pottery-mak-ing may receive attention in art class but is by and large ignored by the school population. The same goes for someone who is a creative writer. Nobody has a pep rally for them.

Not surprisingly, these artists grow accustomed to being alone or out of sync with many of their peers. If you are going to be a part of their world, you, too, may be out of the mainstream, and you need to consider whether that is important to you.

On the other hand, if you and your partner share a mutual level of artistic passion, you may be able to overlook other deficiencies. If you are strong in artistic passion, I can almost guarantee you that your soul mate will be strong in that area as well.

CHAPTER 21

DIMENSION **19** | Values

MOST PEOPLE TEND to hold their values close to their hearts. Certainly you want to be closely aligned with your partner on any strongly held beliefs or convictions, including your attitude toward faith, patriotism, how to raise children, or a host of ethical and character issues. But it is also critical for marital partners to have similar values concerning the everyday essentials of living. For instance, if you have a value that promotes saving money, as opposed to a value of spending money lavishly on yourself, you don't want to marry a person whose value in this area is too dissimilar to yours. As in many of the core values that we have been exploring, the key issue is to be matched closely with someone a lot like you.

Denice and Robert have been going together for more than a year, and they talk constantly about their future marriage. Most of their friends and family members assume that they will be married within a year. I hope not. I think they need much more time and perhaps should not marry at all.

Why? Because they are so dissimilar in the ways they handle money. Denice is a hard worker and earns good money, but she is terrible at saving money. She's never seen a sale at the mall that didn't have something with her name written on it! In her mid-twenties, she has never had a savings account and has never learned to balance her checkbook. She simply writes checks until the bank sends her a notice that she is overdrawn, along with a penalty for bouncing a check. Denice gushes about the wonderful future she and Robert are going to have together, but she takes no steps to help pay for that future by denying herself some expensive trinket and placing a portion of her earnings in savings. She wants a comfortable future, but she also wants to spend money and enjoy life to the fullest right now.

Robert isn't much better when it comes to planning for their future. He, too, is a hard worker, especially since he is laden with debts he incurred while in college. But Robert is a saver. When he gets his paycheck it goes right into the bank, and he is extremely frugal about not spending any more of his earnings than necessary. Even on their dates, Robert tries to do the least expensive things possible. Robert and Denice may be deeply in love, and they may match in many other dimensions, but the area of their values is going to be a problem for them if they don't make some adjustments now. Can a marriage survive a difference in values with regard to money? Yes, but not very well.

Although money problems and money squabbles between marriage partners are almost always symptoms rather than causes, they cannot be ignored. If you and your partner are not similar in your attitudes toward the earning, saving, giving, and spending of money, you are setting yourself up for a lifetime of struggles if you get married.

Maybe one of the reasons money matters so much is that for many people, money means power. The person who controls the purse strings calls the shots. For some people, money means security. For others, it is a means of control. Sometimes it signifies independence. Often it is viewed as a source of status or self-esteem. Notice, all of these issues stem from a person's self-conception and character. The most significant emotional issue related to money is trust:

"Do you really trust me enough to put your money where your mouth is?"

"Does what belongs to you really belong to me?"

"Are we in this thing together?"

Two factors make these questions more complicated for modern singles considering a marriage partner. First, the emphasis on male-female equality in the workplace may have dispelled forever the notion that the husband is to be the provider and the wife is to be protected as the nurturer in the family. Second, because many people are marrying later than in previous generations, and many others are marrying for the second or third time, they often bring to the marriage more financial resources—perhaps a home, a car, a bank account, or investments. Conversely, many are bringing along a house payment, a car payment, an overdrawn checking account, massive credit-card debt, college loans, or poor business investments.

You may be reluctant to admit it, but your money is a reflection of *you*. By this, I mean it is simple to see where your priorities, commitments, and other values lie merely by examining how you earn and spend your money. More than anything, the way we use money reflects our security or insecurities in the area of our self-conception.

In a great marriage, you no longer talk about *my* money and *your* money; you must begin to think, speak, and act in terms of *our* money. The day you say, "I do," you inherit all your partner's assets, debts, and liabilities, if not legally then at least emotionally. Only if you are ready for such a commitment are you ready for marriage.

You should also look carefully at your values concerning social and political issues. If you have a value of caring for needy people, you don't want to be in a relationship with someone who says, "Are you kidding? Those people made their beds; let them lie in them!"

If you have a great concern for environmental issues, you will probably do better in marriage with someone who shares your views. Certainly, every thinking person is in favor of clean air, unpolluted water, and conservation of our natural resources. But if those issues profoundly affect the way you function in everyday life, you'd be better off with someone who shares your values in those areas, rather than spending your life trying to convert your spouse.

Political issues can also be a source of contention. Marylyn and I match extremely well on almost every one of the twenty-nine dimensions, but we don't always see eye-to-eye on politics or political candidates. Would I prefer that she vote for the same people I do? Of course! Would she rather that I vote for her favorite candidates? Naturally. But do we allow those political differences to become divisive in our relationship? Not for long! They do make for some lively conversations at times, and we've had to incorporate our own models for conflict resolution. But we have far too many good things going on in our marriage of more than forty-five years to allow our political views and values to divide us.

That, of course, is the key issue when looking at how similar you are to a potential mate in the area of values orientation. Do you have enough positives in your relationship to overcome any negatives?

CHAPTER 22

DIMENSION **20** | Industry

"I KNEW I HAD FOUND my soul mate," said James, "when I realized what a hard worker Judy is. I'm one of those rare people who actually enjoys working, and yet so many women that I've dated look at work as drudgery. Not Judy. She loves what she does."

If James and Judy are well matched in the other essential components, they are probably going to do well in their marriage. They are definitely a good match in the area of "industry," which basically has to do with a person's attitude and orientation toward work.

Industry is slightly different from energy and ambition. A person could have a lot of energy but spend his or her life outside picking up rocks. If he is also ambitious, he might say, "I'd like to sell these rocks." The person with industry may say, "And if that doesn't work, I will study and become a paleontologist. I will work hard and make something good out of these rocks, regardless of what it takes."

The person with a lot of energy may be out picking up rocks, simply because she is bored and has so much energy she doesn't know what to do with herself. The ambitious person says, "Mmm, maybe there's a way I can use these rocks to get ahead in life, to accomplish my goals." And the industrious person says, "I will do whatever is necessary to succeed in my chosen field of endeavor." The differences are rather subtle, unless you happen to be living with that person! Then if one partner is a hard worker, and the other is always trying to get out of work, or avoids or ignores it, tension is going to be created in the relationship.

I mentioned earlier that Marylyn is an extremely hard worker. She works with me in our offices at eHarmony, and on our days off she works around our house. She's watering the plants, dusting where the cleaning lady has missed, getting the roast ready for dinner, setting the table, or doing whatever needs done around our home. Moreover, she likes the idea that I am a hard worker. She shares my goal to help change the world by helping people to be better matched in marriages. She rarely complains when I have to work late at the office or the taping of one of our eHarmony television or radio spots runs long. We are well matched on industry, and if we weren't, it would be a problem. She'd be looking at me and wondering, *Why isn't that lazy sluggard doing something besides lying around watching the Chicago Cubs?* Either that, or I'd be looking at her, thinking, *What an obsessive workaholic that woman is!*

A lazy person and an industrious person are sure to disagree on many of the basic issues of life, including everything from what time to get up or go to bed, to how to spend weekends or vacations. If you don't think industry matters, wait till you try having a birthday party for one of your children! To ensure the greatest amount of satisfaction in marriage, you should seek to be matched with someone who is very similar to you in the industry dimension.

CHAPTER 23

DIMENSION **21** | Curiosity

SOME PEOPLE ARE naturally curious—it is part of their core personality traits—and they don't have to work at it. They sincerely want to know how things work, why people do the things they do, what makes the difference between success or failure, what something looks, tastes, or feels like. They have a natural inquisitiveness and will ask you a million questions about everything from "What's it like to be a psychotherapist delving into the intimate details and interpersonal relationships of people you hardly know?" to "Neil, why do you always wear a blue shirt in your television commercials?" They are not being snoopy; they honestly are fascinated with the details.

Other people are more content with a broad-brush approach to life. "Honey, the Smiths had a new baby."

"Really? Was it a boy or a girl?"

"Er, ahh . . . I'm not sure, but I know it's a baby!"

If he or she is completely satisfied with just that much information, while the partner is pressing for every juicy detail, it can become a frustrating relationship for both of them. Few things are more defeating for a person with a high level of curiosity than to express heartfelt interest in something and then to hear the response "I don't know." Or, "What difference does it make? Who cares?"

"Who cares? I care! Don't you?"

No, he doesn't. He's not being mean or rude; he's just not wired as you are. And that can create tension in a marriage. Remember, your goal is to match with someone who harmonizes the best in the most areas of life that really matter.

Marylyn and I are both extremely curious. Interestingly, though, her curiosity tends to look up and mine looks down. We'll be passing by a neighborhood and she'll say, "Oh, look at the progress they are making on that new house up on the hill." Meanwhile, my attention is much lower. "Yes, that's great," I say, "but did you notice they still haven't fixed that brick on the curb?" We both have curiosity, but it does not need to be about the same things.

Marylyn satisfies some of her curiosity about the broader world by reading newspapers and news magazines from cover to cover. I mean, she *reads* the paper, every page of it! Me? I check out the headlines, the top news items on the front page, a few features, and then I turn to what really matters—the sports pages. Marylyn reads for information; I read for entertainment.

On the other hand, Marylyn is much more reserved around people she doesn't know well, and I'm usually inviting them to dinner by the time we take the elevator together down from the eleventh floor to the ground floor.

Having dissimilar amounts of curiosity would not necessarily be a deal breaker in a relationship, but it is something to consider seriously. Our research at eHarmony convinces me that most people will enjoy greater marital satisfaction if they relate more easily in this dimension.

CHAPTER 24

DIMENSION **22** | Vitality and Security

At eHARMONY we've conducted numerous studies about what men and women really want in a partner. Again and again, the results come back the same: Men want women who look healthy and vital; women want men who can offer security.

As we've noted earlier, physical appearance always ranks high on what men and women want in a partner. Yet, in seventeen cross-cultural studies done around the world, the number one quality men seek is "fertility." But wait a minute! Fertility relates to having babies or the ability to have babies, and we know that many formerly married people do not in fact want to have more children! Do men really want women who have the quality of fertility? Or do they merely want a woman who looks as though she could have a child? Because of that, we've recognized that what men actually want is a woman who looks vital, healthy, and is in good shape physically.

"I am not naive," said Bradley, a moderately good-looking man in his mid-thirties who carries a slight paunch around his middle. "I know that I'm not a hunk, and I understand that the fashion model look is unrealistic for most people. For starters, most models are over six feet tall, and I'm only five foot nine! So I've tried to lower my expectations. The woman I want to spend my life with doesn't have to look like a model, but I would like her to be attractive enough to hold my attention."

Women, on the other hand, desire men who can provide security for them. A woman wants a man who will help her to create a home in which she can feel safe; a lifestyle in which she can have and raise children in a healthy, secure environment; and she doesn't want to have to worry about where the food, clothing, or rent money is coming from. If this reminds you of the traditional role of the husband as provider and protector of the home, you are absolutely correct. Despite repeated attempts to convince women that they can find all the fulfillment they need outside the home, that position has not sold and we have stacks of statistical analyses to prove it. Most women still want a man who can provide economic, emotional, and physical security, especially during the childbearing years. Interestingly, this desire doesn't change greatly even among women who have achieved outstanding success in their careers.

Brenda is a successful trial lawyer who lives and works in New York City. She earns a comfortable six-figure income, does not need a man to validate her existence, and is quite candid about the fact that she is picky, that she has high requirements of the man she is looking for on eHarmony. "Giving up my autonomy in marriage is not frightening to me; I honestly believe that I would relish the opportunity to meld my life with my soul mate's, to rest and relax in the arms of a man I could trust. But placing my economic security in the hands of anyone else has always bothered me. The man I marry needn't be wealthy, but he must be capable of providing a sense of security in our personal lives."

Most women also prefer men with whom they can be "emotionally naked" —secure enough in the relationship to be vulnerable and expose their deepest thoughts, dreams, hopes, and desires without fear of condemnation or humiliation. "He doesn't have to agree with how I feel," commented Maria, "but he does have to care."

Women also want to feel physically protected. That doesn't mean if your partner is not a bodybuilder, policeman, or firefighter you are mismatched, but most every woman wants to know that if accosted, insulted, or threatened in any way—whether on a dark city street or at a company Christmas party—her husband will not stand by idly and watch her get hurt. He may not be a physically strong man, but he will have the courage to do whatever is possible to prevent her from physical injury, abuse, or pain.

Being matched in the areas of vitality and security requires that you be absolutely honest about your personal tastes and your emotional needs. If you feel strongly that you need a healthy, attractive spouse, please be straightforward to admit that it's a priority to you. Likewise, if you know that you couldn't possibly live with a person who cannot provide the security you need, you are fooling yourself to think you can be happy in a long-term relationship with that person. Remember, these things run deep down into our core values. They are not likely to change, so if you are not satisfied with that person now, you will be much less satisfied with him or her twenty years from now. On the other hand, if this person matches up well with what you know you need, it will bring tremendous peace and confidence into your life.

CHAPTER 25

DIMENSION **23** | Autonomy Versus Closeness

THE LAST OF OUR core dimensions—those components of a good relationship that are relatively hard to change—is the desire for autonomy versus closeness. Some people love solitude; others loathe it. Many people enjoy being alone and can handle it much better than others. They can work for hours in isolation, not talking with anyone or interacting a great deal with the outside world. They enjoy long stretches of silence to think or study and meditate on what matters to them. Many artistic and creative people fall into this category. That same sense of aloneness carries over into their personal relationships. If you are in a relationship with this sort of person, he doesn't want you to be with him everywhere he goes. She may prefer that you work outside the home rather than in a home office. He doesn't want you to be hanging all over him in public and perhaps not even in private.

On the other hand, some people are natural extroverts—they not only want to be around people a lot; they need to be around people, especially you! She can't get enough of you; she wants you with her all the time; she's a high-maintenance woman and you are perpetually on call.

But you don't have to be an outgoing person to desire to spend as much time as possible with your partner. That's all part of falling in love!

OTHER PEOPLE ARE more introverted. It requires enormous effort and energy for them to function with groups of people. She may love spending close time with her partner, but she also needs time by herself.

After a party, Dave goes off by himself to read or simply to rest. Give him an hour or two to recharge his "emotional batteries" and he will be fine, but if he is continually thrust into situations where he must be close with other people, he becomes increasingly agitated. His partner, Marlene, loves to have Dave around all the time, but she has learned to give Dave time to recharge after they are together in public. It takes an understanding attitude on both their parts to make the relationship work well.

If your partner is the kind of person who "needs a lot of space," that's fine, but if you need him or her to be there for you on a regular basis, it could spell trouble in your relationship.

Other people prefer their autonomy simply because they do not like being accountable to anyone. They want to come and go as they please, to be able to jump into the car or onto a plane and be somewhere else on a whim. Again, there's nothing wrong with that, unless you happen to be married to a person who wants you to be in close proximity. Although one has to wonder why you would consider marriage at all if you desire to operate unilaterally in life.

Granted, some couples function better with a little "breathing room"; they don't do everything together; they show up at social functions at different times, sometimes driving separate cars, and they still are happily married. They don't require the same level of closeness in their relationship that others do. But others need to be holding hands every time they walk more than a few feet in the same direction; they need to eat two to three meals per day together, to see each other's faces, to speak to each other often throughout the day.

As in other core dimensions, the details may vary but what matters the most is that you and your partner are similar in what you want and need in the areas of autonomy versus closeness. If you need more closeness in the relationship and your partner desires more autonomy, you must be sure that most of the other dimensions are extremely strong. If there is too much discrepancy in this regard, you may even need to reevaluate whether you two are to be together at all. Our studies indicate that the best marriages involve people who have a similar need to be alone or a similar need for more closeness. Remember, these are core dimensions. They don't usually change without a huge amount of effort and, usually, they don't change at all. People change, but not much.

Skills That Can Be Developed

EVERYONE BRINGS to a relationship a "package" of personality traits, values, expectations, and goals. Some of these, as we've seen, are genetic; others are ingrained through education or environment; many of these core traits are relatively difficult to change. But there are other dimensions that should be considered in a good relationship, and these qualities are skills that can be learned or improved throughout your life. The best marriages are made up of two individuals who are similar in these dimensions. Let's look at Group 3: Skills That Can Be Developed.

CHAPTER 26

DIMENSION **24** | Communication

THE U.S. GOVERNMENT and the governments of several other nations, as well as many churches and social organizations, have recognized the high cost of divorce to the fabric of society as well as in dollars and cents. They have decided that it is in everyone's interest to help people enjoy better marriages and family relationships. Consequently, these groups are pouring millions of dollars and thousands of man-hours into programs designed to help couples develop skills that will help them cope with the stresses and strains of marriage.

I applaud these efforts, but I'm convinced that we can do more for people by helping them to be better matched before going into marriage rather than trying to repair messes after the fact. This is especially true in the areas of communication, conflict resolution, and sociability. Because it is so vital for a good relationship, let's take a closer look at deep communication.

You've probably heard someone say, "Communication is the lifeblood of a great marriage." And it is, but what does that really mean? How can you become a communication expert, choose a mate well, and maintain the magic after your wedding day? What are some concrete steps you can take to assess your communication skills and improve them?

Good communication requires three active efforts on the part of the individuals involved:

1. They need to be able to get a sense of what is going on in their bodies and minds, and they need to get into the habit of putting those feelings into words. "This is what I'm feeling right now" is a

statement you need to keep handy at all times. "This is what I think . . ." and "This is what I have experienced . . ." are helpful expressions as well.

Most of us walk around with all sorts of thoughts, secrets, intuitions, and feelings trapped inside us. We know better, but we act as though other people can read our minds. This is especially true in dating and marriage relationships. Someone simply assumes that the other person understands what the other person is thinking or feeling. The key to good communication is to allow somebody in on those thoughts. To truly get to know one another, you and your partner must find a way to express what is going on inside you and learn how to hear and receive each other's thoughts and feelings accurately.

Your relationship will work best if you find that the thoughts and feelings you have experienced and the thoughts and feelings your partner has expressed overlap so much that you start saying, "Do you feel that, too? I thought I was the only person in the world who felt that way. Do you think that, too?" That is when communication leads to intimacy. Intimacy, of course, can be defined in various ways but, basically, intimacy takes place in those areas where you and your partner overlap.

Generally speaking, men have much more difficulty in expressing what is going on inside of them than do women. Part of this is simply the way we are wired, but to a great extent our society teaches men from the time they are little boys to hold in their emotions, thoughts, and feelings. "Don't cry; you're a big boy." "Keep it to yourself." "Hold your cards close to the vest." "Never let them see you sweat." Boys, young men, and adult men are inundated with statements such as these, most of which are ludicrous and counterproductive when it comes to communication.

It's almost as though there has been a conspiracy against boys in our society, thwarting any efforts that might help them get inside their heads and get in touch with their thoughts and their feelings. We don't want our boys to be effeminate, so we encourage boys to pick up a bat and swing it at a ball. We would never want the boy to cry, because "that's a sign of weakness, and men must be strong." Oh? He's getting tired of playing with a bat and a ball? Here is a bigger ball. You can teach him how to shoot this ball through a basket, and that will keep him from getting too far inside himself. If he doesn't like that, we have a cylindrical ball and he can learn how to throw it in a spiral, or tote it across some white lines. But whatever you do, don't let that boy get inside his head! We don't want him to get in touch with any of those softer emotions or weak feelings that he may have.

Now, please understand, I am a big sports fan. I may be one of the world's most avid Chicago Cubs fans and have been most of my life. (Do you have any idea how painful this has been at times?) I enjoy watching the UCLA Bruins sporting events as well. But if we teach boys to hit a baseball, or toss a basketball, or run with a football, and never teach them how to express what is in their hearts and minds, or how to express what they are feeling, we are handicapping them for life!

As a rule, girls do much better at this. When they are as young as twelve or thirteen, they are on the telephone or computer with their friends, expressing their thoughts, feelings, and emotions. "Did you see what he did? I felt like falling down on my face! I thought I was going to die, I was so embarrassed." As much as it often drives parents bonkers that the girls are on the telephone so much, it is good that they have opportunities to express their thoughts and feelings. Many of them are quite good at it by the time they become adults. Certainly, there are some women who have trouble in this area, and some men are excellent at it but, in general, most women are better at expressing their feelings than most men.

Often in therapy I'll ask a man, "Do you want to make your marriage a lot better, real fast?"

"Oh, yeah, Doc. Can you give me a pill for that?"

"No, but I can give you a simple secret that can transform your relationship."

"Really? Go ahead. Hit me."

"Okay, you can revolutionize your relationship with that woman if you will simply figure out what is going on inside you and then learn how to express it in words in an accurate way."

"That's it? That's all? Do you really think that will make a difference?"

"Guaranteed."

"I can do that!"

And he can. If he does it, she will think she has a new man! But it may take some time and practice. As one fellow put it, "I'm not too good at love out loud."

But you can be, and in a good relationship you must be good at expressing your innermost thoughts and feelings.

There is not a woman in the world who doesn't enjoy having a man tell her what is going on inside his head. Why? Because that is how she gets to know him. This is how they begin to weave the fabric of their relationship, weaving *him* and *her* together so there is a *them*. That is what love is all about.

Women can help men be better at expressing their feelings. Most guys will give you the facts. "I got fired today." But if you really want to know what is going on inside, you may have to probe much deeper to get him to open up and tell you how he is feeling about being fired. The best way to do this is to ask direct questions: "How does getting fired make you feel? Are you angry? Feeling incompetent, unjustly treated, inadequate, relieved?" He probably won't tell you unless you ask for more information, and even then you may have to drag it out of him. But if you have a future together, it will be worth the effort.

Don't wait for a crisis, though, before attempting to express your feelings. One of the best things that happened in the early part of Marylyn's and my relationship took place during a cross-country drive. As we were motoring along one night, Marylyn said to me, "Neil, just tell me about you."

Nobody in my entire life had ever asked me to do that. It was the most stunning thing she could have said to me! I told her a little about myself, probably about twenty-six seconds' worth.

She said, "Tell me more; tell me more!"

We talked for about two hours. During most of that conversation, Marylyn was introducing me to my private inside world by having me talk about myself. It was such an incredible gift, not only to me, but to our marriage. Over time, I recognized how important that kind of talk was to our marriage. I also recognized how important it was for me. You can do well in communicating with a person of the opposite sex when you get in touch with yourself and learn how to put words to your thoughts and feelings. That is not the easiest thing for many men to do, but the payoff is well worth the investment.

For singles, communication is an important diagnostic device in figuring out whether a particular person is a good match for you. I've seen so many people in therapy who didn't get this squared away before the wedding day, and they went ahead and married somebody that doesn't have the capacity to communicate or hasn't taken an interest in cultivating the skill. They come into the counseling office and say, "Dr. Warren, what is wrong with us? We love each other. Why isn't our marriage working?"

If you want to infuse your relationship with something that is going to take it the distance, develop this capacity to express yourself. Be in touch with what is going on within you, and be willing to honestly express those feelings to another person.

2. The second skill a couple must have or learn is hearing and understanding the other person. Imagine, for instance, that you are talking to your potential partner and you've been having a bad day. You say something like this: "I'm just feeling a little down today."

He says, "Really? I'm sorry to hear that. Do you want to go to the ball game?" Or maybe he says, "Really? What's wrong? Tell me about it. Are you physically sick or maybe just a little blue? What's going on?"

In the second response, the person is listening to you and trying to accurately understand. He's not attempting to bypass the communication process, simply looking for a quick fix or totally ignoring your problem to get on to what he wants to do. Real communication involves a desire to know what is going on and a willingness to invest the time and effort to do so.

The better you get at listening to somebody else, the greater the chances of that person feeling that he or she has been heard, understood, and known, and as a result will feel closer to you. In every sphere of life, you will draw a lot of people to yourself if you simply get good at listening. Theodore Reik called it "listening with the third ear." By that he meant being able to listen to not just the words in a conversation, but listening as if you are panning for gold, dipping down into that river of emotions and finding a tiny golden nugget. Then you lift the nugget out of all the verbiage and hand it back to the person as you say, "Is this how you feel? Is this what I am hearing?"

They may look back at you in wide-eyed amazement and say, "Yeah! You are the first person that really gets it."

And you have. That is real communication.

In your search for a soul mate, make sure that you find a person who is not only good at talking, but is also good at listening to you. That makes intimacy possible.

The third aspect of good communication is the ability to accurately understand the meaning of what your partner is saying, and to be able to repeat it back to him or her for clarification and then dig deeper. If you want to be sure the person you are considering for marriage is the right person, strive to engage in deep communication, not merely superficial conversation. This sort of deep communication is extremely important to singles, since it is only as you get involved in talking and listening to a person that you begin to sense whether the two of you really belong together. When you find that person who will talk with you and listen to you, and you do the same with him or her, you recognize, "We are a great match for each other!" What you are really discovering are the areas where the two of you overlap, which, if the relationship proceeds toward marriage, will lead to heightened intimacy.

Surely there are times when you talk with another person, and the more carefully you listen, the more you realize, *This person is very different from me. I don't belong with this person at all.* That's okay, as long as this is not a person you are thinking about being with for the rest of your life. But when it is a person with whom you are going to have all things in common, it is crucial that you find out whether the two of you are at similar points in the ability and desire to communicate.

Years ago, before I was married, I met an attractive woman on an airplane. As we talked, we discovered that we had very different approaches to a number of things. For instance, we talked about children. She saw children as being inconvenient until they got to be three or four years old. I didn't feel that way at all. The more we talked, the more I recognized that we were too different. We didn't really belong together. It didn't take months of dating to figure that out, just a willingness to communicate on a level deeper than a surface conversation.

Marylyn and I both see children as so important. We both have the same deep sense of ambition to do something meaningful in the world. As we got to know one another and began sharing our inner thoughts and feelings, we realized that we are very much alike in all the places that matter most to us.

The things that matter the most are usually the things down at the center of the person. In a good relationship, it is extremely important that you and your partner overlap on those things, if indeed you are thinking about a long-term relationship. The only way you can get to whether or not you overlap on those things is to develop good communication skills. People who aren't good at communication leave too many questions in the air. "Do we really overlap at the center of ourselves?"

"I don't know. He's never talked very much to me."

"I don't know how to listen very well to her."

On the other hand, you may find yourself saying something such as, "Wow, when I put words to my feelings and express them, and he catches the meaning, receives it, and then says something about himself and I receive it, I feel that we are really getting to know one another." Of course, what you hope for is to be able to say, "We're a lot alike."

To have a successful marriage, you and your partner must have a similar desire to communicate, a willingness to continually work at communication, and the ability to do so. When both partners maintain the interest in good communication and the skills to keep going deeper with one another, there is no end to the depth of love that can be experienced in marriage.

CHAPTER 27

DIMENSION **25** | Conflict Resolution

WHEN I WROTE the book *Learning to Live with the Love of Your Life,* we solicited assistance from prominent people across the United States. "Tell us the number one best marriage that you know of," we requested. They responded enthusiastically, and we found one hundred great marriages from all over America. We gave long survey questionnaires to each individual within these marriages. Interestingly, more than ninety of these one hundred first-class marriages said, "We have a lot of conflict."

Our findings validated a principle I had observed as a professional therapist. When you see a great marriage, often the two people are unique, lively personalities, and they have opinions or practices that vary from each other's. They experience disagreements over these differences, but the effort they put forth to work through their conflict actually makes their relationship stronger and both of them better people. When two people share their deepest thoughts and feelings, even when they know their partner may not agree on every point, it always moves the relationship forward.

That's why I tell people, "Don't run away from conflict. Learn to deal with it."

In a good relationship both partners must be good at resolving conflicts. As we noted in our discussion of anger, nobody is exempt from conflicts—not even people with great marriages—but those who do best in marriage are the couples who learn how to resolve disputes before they say, "I do." If you are going to marry well, you must learn to deal with conflicts, how to understand them, how to manage them, and how you can make them work for you instead of against you.

You can't resolve a conflict by ignoring it, sweeping it under the rug, or pretending that it doesn't exist. Just because a conflict is dormant, don't assume it is dead. Unresolved conflicts have an extremely high rate of resurrection. An unresolved conflict usually will be resuscitated at the most inopportune time, when the pressure is on in some other area of the relationship.

The reason we place conflict resolution among those dimensions that can be improved is because it is both an *attitude* and a *skill* that can be learned. I'm convinced that conflict resolution can be easily learned by any individual or couple that wants to do so. But you must want to! If you or your partner is unwilling to work at it, your relationship will suffer horrendous strain and possibly will not survive. Conflict resolution is crucial to your future.

I've always liked the fact that Marylyn feels free to disagree with me, to say, "No, Neil, that isn't how I see that issue at all." But our differences of opinion can cause conflict. It doesn't threaten our relationship, or cause us to love each other less, or dislike each other somehow. In fact, it usually engenders deeper, more thoughtful discussions between us. Marylyn might say something such as, "I don't quite agree with your position on that issue, but tell me more about why you feel that way. And then I would like to tell you what I think about it."

If you and your partner disagree occasionally, that is not cause to throw in the towel and give up on your relationship. It is only when two people have freedom in relationship to each other that true harmony begins to happen. But if you have two people who suppress their feelings, or otherwise lose their freedom in relationship to each other, it isn't long until they are seething, screeching, or scratching at the door wanting to get out.

I encourage couples to use a five-point model to help manage conflicts. When you are considering somebody as a potential long-term mate and you disagree about something, that's fine. That is point number one of our five-point model: Conflict happens, and that is okay. As much as we talk about similarities at eHarmony and matching you with someone who is a lot like you, it is not necessary that your thoughts and feelings and those of your partner align perfectly all the time. It is all right to have occasional conflicts, and it is safe to acknowledge that as you attempt to resolve the problem.

Grace and Lanny have been dating for more than a year, and they seem to get along fine in most areas, except one. "Grace thinks that any cultured person should enjoy and appreciate opera," said Lanny, "and I think, *Why would I want to waste my time at the opera? I don't appreciate it, I don't understand it, and often it is in a different language.* We have an ongoing conflict over that. She wants me to appreciate opera, and I have no desire to do so." Lanny and Grace need to know that having a disagreement over opera is okay.

Second, conflict resolution will work best if Grace has the chance to fully explain why she feels so strongly about the opera and Lanny has a chance to fully explain why he feels equally as strong about his dislike of opera. They both need to be *heard* completely; they need to understand and appreciate each other's position on this issue. They do not have to like the position of their partner or agree with it, but it's important that they understand it.

Sometimes it's difficult to understand why your partner thinks or feels a certain way, and you may not want to discuss it, but you must at least try to accept the fact that he feels as he does. An ancient adage says, "Seek first to understand before being understood."

Third, you must pinpoint precisely what you disagree about. Maybe Lanny and Grace's fight isn't about the fact that everybody should appreciate opera. Perhaps what they are really squabbling about is that the opera is on Friday night, and so is the baseball game that Lanny wants to attend. Maybe the crux of the matter is that every time there is a choice between baseball and opera, Grace wants to go to the opera.

What can Lanny do? He can start by saying, "You know, Grace, I don't know anything about opera, and when you say that I ought to like it, I feel sort of insulted. To me, it's as though you are saying any truly intelligent person would love the opera, and since I don't, I'm a lesser person. That hurts me."

Or possibly Grace and Lanny's spat has more to do with money than it does music. Opera tickets can be expensive or hard to get. Whatever it is, you must be specific so you both know where the real issue lies.

Fourth, Grace and Lanny must come to the place where they can both compromise for the good of the relationship. Grace can say, "Okay, Lanny, how can I give, and how can you give so we can be together on this?"

Lanny may say, "I admit that I don't like opera very much, but I also have to admit that I don't know much about it. But because you do like it, I'll agree to see if I can develop a taste for it. I'll go with you to three operas. But after those three operas, grant me the right to say, 'I still don't get it. I don't like it that much, and I prefer to do something else.'"

"Sure, that seems fair," Grace might reply. The two of them have done a good job of resolving that conflict. They have struck a compromise that is comfortable to both of them.

Fifth, at that point, because they have been able to resolve a conflict, minor as it may seem, Grace and Lanny should congratulate each other. In any relationship, whether it is a dating relationship, a friendship, or a business deal, when two people encounter something on which they disagree and they can work out a compromised resolution to that conflict, those two people have done something valuable for their long-term relationship. They need to say, "Nice going." When Marylyn and I resolve a conflict, I just hold my hand up and she slaps my hand with a "high five." What we are saying is, "We are getting pretty good at this, aren't we?" And it draws us together because each of us has the sense that we are appreciated by the other person. Beyond that, those brief mini-celebrations give us confidence for the future. "We made it through that tough spot. We can make it through others."

I'm convinced that most couples will experience conflict at times. But whether the conflict is helpful or harmful to their relationship usually comes down to one main factor—*respect*. Do these two people have mutual respect for each other? If they do, I'm confident that the conflict can draw them closer together; if they don't, it is going to take a major repair job to make that house a home.

What makes the difference? Usually selfishness. Conflict that is destructive frequently centers around one person's preoccupation with his or her own needs. It's that old "I want what I want when I want it" syndrome, and it is almost always counterproductive to a relationship.

Some individuals decide to deal with conflict by denying it exists, pretending that everything is always okay . . . all the time. Maybe his parents never disagreed in front of other family members, or possibly her parents fought all the time when she was a little girl and the last thing she wants in her relationship with a man is conflict. Better to just keep quiet and go with the flow.

NO, it isn't!

Many people falsely assume that conflict should be managed the way Mom and Dad dealt with it. But a lot of parents hid their conflicts from their children, so the kids got the impression that their mom and dad never had any conflict at all, which is probably an extremely inaccurate assessment. More important, though, the children never saw a model of how to resolve conflict in the home.

My mom and dad, for instance, never fought; they never argued. Whenever they had a disagreement, my mom just poured herself into her crocheting, and Dad got quiet and read his newspaper. Either that, or he'd go off to his business and stay there fourteen hours a day. They didn't have any conflict that I could see. I never once heard them speak harshly to each other, but the conflict was real nonetheless and was steering their relationship.

Other people attempt to deal with conflicts by manipulating their partner through guilt, flattery, subtle threats or even blackmail, or other sorts of deal-making. "I'll do this for you, if you'll do that for me." All of these manipulations are simply a person's attempts to get his or her own way. Manipulation is consistently a negative in a relationship; it is a sign of disrespect. Somebody is trying to rob someone of his or her dignity.

But when two people respect themselves and each other and are more concerned about resolving the conflict than winning a personal battle, there's hope. You can tell whether a person respects himself or herself by the way he expresses his opinions with a calm assurance, or the way she asks questions or requests clarifications of what has been stated. You can tell if two people respect each other by the way they listen to one another, sincerely trying to understand what is being said. Watch, too, for facial expressions. Sometimes a person may say all the right things, but her facial expressions more accurately reveal the truth.

Five Helpful Hints for Dealing with Conflict

In any conflict, try to keep these five simple tips in mind that we saw in Grace and Lanny's dispute over the opera, and you will manage your anger in a more constructive manner.

1. *Allow each other the freedom to think and feel honestly.* It does little good for you to tell your partner, "Well, you shouldn't feel that way!"

He does! And that is his prerogative. Your telling him how he should or shouldn't feel is irrelevant. Accept the fact that a conflict exists and your partner is angry and has a legitimate right to feel the way he or she does, even if you disagree with that assessment of the situation.

2. *It's more important to be heard and understood than to win.* This is a critical point that often goes out the window when couples engage in conflict resolution. We all want to get our points across, but if we merely get our point out there into the air, so what? Until your partner understands what you have said, you have not communicated. Likewise, until you understand what your partner has said, you have not really listened. One oft-suggested means of making sure that real communication is taking place while you are trying to resolve a conflict is to restate your partner's position. "Let me see if I understand what you are saying. You believe that we are not spending enough time together in private. Is that correct?"

On the other hand, if you know that your partner has understood your thoughts and feelings, you will maintain a closeness even if you continue to disagree on the issue in point.

3. *Clarify your points of disagreement.* When we get in arguments, most of us tend to simply repeat our contentions over and over. Determine to at least agree about what the two of you are disagreeing about! That may seem much simpler than it actually is. Most conflicts start over something minor, but the real issue lurks somewhere below the surface. That's the point you want to get resolved.

When conflicts break out, it's easy to get sidetracked onto other issues. Early in our marriage, Marylyn and I used to get into many conflicts where I would end up saying something such as, "You know, you remind me so much of your mother when you are like that!"

"*My* mother? What about *your* mother?" she'd retort, and before long, we were talking about mothers when we started out having a disagreement about where we were going to go on vacation! We needed to get clear regarding the conflict we were trying to resolve— that she wanted to go on vacation in June to a place where some of our neighbors vacation at that time, and I wanted to go in August to a place where we could enjoy being alone. When conflicts occur, you must stick to the issue if you hope to obtain any real resolution.

4. *Maintain an attitude of give and take.* Look for ways you can compromise in the conflict without compromising your integrity. It helps to actually state that to your partner so he or she knows that you are searching for a solution together rather than simply proving you are right and the other person is wrong. The key is to remain cooperative rather than combative.

5. *When you resolve a conflict—regardless of how small—pat yourselves on the back* and if possible celebrate with some reward. You've accomplished something significant in your relationship. Congratulate each other and let the other person know how happy you are to feel understood and to know that your feelings are considered.

One of the keys to resolving conflict is to disarm it of its explosive power. Similar to cutting off the fuse on a lit stick of dynamite, the conflict is still there, but you have defused it long enough to be dealt with.

My colleague Les Parrott suggests that one way of doing this is to use what he calls the "X-Y-Z formula." Rather than hurling personal insults at your partner, alienating him or her further, distill your point so you can say something like this: "In situation X, when you do Y, I feel Z."

Suddenly, you are no longer talking about personal failures on the part of your partner, inadequacies, or mistakes. You are talking about your *feelings*. That little phrase "X Y Z" may be enough to spin the conflict around. "In situation X, when you do Y, I feel Z." Here's how it sounds in real life:

"When we are driving down the road, and you turn the radio station without asking me first, I feel like I don't even matter to you." Did you follow the progression? "In situation X, when you do Y, I feel Z." That is very different from saying, "Who made you king of the radio?" That sort of comment will be contemptuous to your partner and will inevitably inflame a conflict.

Les also suggests that couples "rate the intensity of feelings" about an issue on a scale of one to ten. When you recognize that you and your partner are upset, simply ask yourself, *Is this an eight for me or is it a three for me?*

Then ask your partner to rate the level of conflict. "You are coming on like gangbusters; this must be an eight or a nine for you, huh?"

In reality, the level of the conflict may not be anywhere near that intensity in your partner's mind. Again, it helps to clarify. That's not always easy to do in the middle of a conflict, but you both might be saved a lot of grief if you can stop just long enough to ask, "What number is this for you?"

Your partner responds, "This is a nine to me!"

Okay, at least you know what level of importance this issue has to him or her, and you can fall back on the five helpful hints for getting it resolved. Whatever you do, don't allow any form of conflict to go by unnoticed or unacknowledged. For instance, if you see that your partner has suddenly gotten quiet while eating dinner, it is important to recognize that. You may say something such as, "I'm not sure, but was there something I said or did that caused you to become so quiet? Help me with that, please."

Try to bring potentially hidden land mines to the surface so you can at least deal with them in the light. As soon as you both are aware that something is wrong or has been hurtful, begin to take steps to start fixing it.

When to Walk Away

Are there times when a person should walk away from a relationship because there are too many conflicts? Absolutely! While some conflict can be good in a relationship, life is no fun when you engage in one battle after another. If you are having one of those intense conflicts more than every three or four days, you should start wondering, *Is this something I want to live with for the rest of my life?*

At that point, you are probably not dealing with conflict so much as one of the other screening dimensions, such as character disorders or emotional red flags. "I love Scott," Leanne said, "and I recognize that we do have a lot of conflict—something sets us off nearly every day—but I think that it's going to get better. Once we are married, I think I can help him and, somehow, we are going to get through that stuff."

As much as my heart goes out to Leanne, she has to wake up and see the truth. She is deluded by her own romantic fallacy that says, "If I get this man and we are married, I just know that he won't be so difficult to get along with."

Guard your heart and mind against that sort of thinking. While a little conflict may be good, you don't want that much tension in your relationship. Some people are simply abrasive. They will find fault with anything. You don't want to live around somebody like that. You don't mind some friction periodically, but you don't want to have regular conflicts that test your soul every step you take.

The same warning applies if you keep having the same conflict over and over again. That conflict is not being resolved. Either your positions have become so entrenched that you are at an impasse and you need to seek outside help, or one or both of you are not ready for a long-term relationship due to a lack of ability to resolve conflicts.

In a good relationship, the number of conflicts should go down over time. As you gain more confidence and trust in each other, knowing that conflicts will not be ignored but that you will both make a conscious attempt to resolve them, the little things are dealt with before they can burrow beneath the surface or blow up into bigger issues.

When new conflicts occur, a well-matched couple isn't shaken. They've been down that road, and they know what to do. They have confidence in their mutual ability to bring the conflict under control.

Often the best time to talk about conflicts is when you don't have any. Perhaps you are enjoying a stimulating conversation about your families, and part of that can include how your parents dealt with conflict. That's a good time to set some guidelines in your relationship about how you are going to manage conflict.

Unfortunately, about 65 percent of all poorly managed conflict happens when one or both partners are under the influence of alcohol or fatigue. If one or both of you have had alcohol to drink, that is not the time to try to deal with a conflict. Back away.

Similarly, if the two of you are terribly tired, that is not a time to deal with conflict. When you are dealing with conflict, you need the full working potential of your brain. You will need some creativity, because problem solving will be involved if you are going to resolve conflict well. That is why it is important to talk about conflict when you are at your best, when you don't have conflicts. During the calm times, when you are coasting down the tranquil river of your relationship, set some systems in place, some guidelines that will help you to navigate the tumultuous white-water rapids you will inevitability be traveling together. Preparing ahead of time will make for a much more enjoyable trip!

As you prepare to meet your soul mate, it will be important for you to examine how any potential partner handles disagreements and conflict. If there is a strong commitment to harmony and maintaining the authenticity of both individuals in the relationship, that is a good sign. Certainly, two people in any close relationship will experience differences of opinion. But if you can't listen to, understand, and appreciate each other's opinions, watch out. On the other hand, don't run away too quickly. You should always strive to deal with conflict rather than ignore it. Admit when you are wrong and, equally important, acknowledge when your partner is right; but most of all, seek for a sense of comfort in the relationship that allows you to broach difficult subjects and issues without having to feel defensive or awkward.

Keep the communication lines free of debris such as bitterness, resentment, or any other leftover residue from anger or conflict. I sincerely believe that conflict is the price we pay for a deeper level of intimacy. If you know how to resolve conflicts well, they can actually bring the two of you closer together. The better you feel about your ability to handle conflicts as a couple, the better you can feel about the potential of your relationship.

CHAPTER 28

DIMENSION **26** | Sociability

"**D**O WE HAVE TO GO OUT with Blake and Laurie again?" Ethan said with a grimace. "We just went to that concert with them two weeks ago. Can't we do something by ourselves?"

"I thought you liked Blake and Laurie," Diane said.

"I do, but it's not as if they are family!"

"Ethan, you're just being silly."

"Maybe so, but I'd rather be with you than with anyone else."

"Oh, Ethan, you are so romantic!"

IS ETHAN REALLY SO ROMANTIC, or is he merely selfish and unsociable? That is a key question Diane will need to answer before going much further in that relationship. The degree to which two people want interpersonal relationships, pursue them, and do well with them needs to be similar if they are going to be matched well enough for marriage.

For instance, some people thrive on being with groups of people, while others prefer to be alone or with one person. She'd rather go out dancing, and he'd prefer that the two of them stay home and watch a movie on television. Of course, too much aloneness can spawn jealousy and possessiveness, which smother the other partner's personality. What should you do if you find yourself in a relationship with a person who may have a lot going for himself or herself, but wants exclusive rights to your time?

In short, back away. That "smothering love" is almost always indicative that something is askew inside the person. An overly possessive person does not feel secure; he or she doesn't possess that profound sense of significance we considered earlier. They are look-ing for you to meet their security needs and make them feel bet-ter about themselves. Possessiveness is almost always something that you need to meet head on and say, "Something is wrong here, and it needs to be taken care of before progressing any further in this relationship."

Don't marry a person that is overly possessive. You may think, *Oh, isn't it wonderful? She wants to be with me all the time; he loves me so much, he doesn't want to be with anyone else.* Such obsessive behavior may even be endearing for a short period of time. But be careful; it may be a neurotic contract that you are forming with this person.

Roger gets upset when Amy wants to go out with her friends or visit with her family members. "Why don't you spend that time with me?" he whines. "What's the matter? Don't you love me?"

Bonnie sulks and complains every time Rod plays golf with his buddies on Saturday rather than spending it with her going to flea markets.

Neither of those is a healthy relationship.

You may be thinking, *But I am so in love with this person, I want to be with her every single second of every minute. And when I am not with her, I feel bereft, empty, and lonely. Why does she have to go to that meeting at her church tonight?*

Whenever I hear that kind of talk, I think, *Oh, that sounds as though he is crowding the relationship.* He's smothering her, and if he is not careful, he may indeed damage any chance they have of being to-gether.

Certainly, there is a developmental period during the early dating days, a phase that a couple goes through when they are falling in love and they can hardly stand being apart from each other. She thinks about him throughout the day; he can't get her face out of his mind. Early in the relationship, they want to have their hand in the other person's hand, and their arms perpetually around the other person's body. They just love being next to each other. "Let me smell your hair a little longer." It's hard to say good night. "Oh, I hate leaving you . . . tomorrow just can't come soon enough." That is a normal and won-derful part of being in love. But if you do not outgrow that sort of cloying togetherness, it would be wise to take a closer look at your relationship. In a mature, growing relationship, you should see signs of becoming more secure. Even though you love your partner, you don't have to have that person around you all the time.

On the other end of the spectrum is the person who has too many friendly relationships, particularly with friends of the opposite sex. Donna worries, "I have fallen for him, but he has all these other girlfriends out there. They still go out to dinner every so often, and I don't know how to handle that. Should I be jealous? Should I be concerned? Is this a serious issue?"

My stock answer to such questions is: "If you think you should be jealous, maybe you *should* be jealous." In other words, if your partner is giving too much attention to someone else, or is doing something that he or she knows bothers you or raises your suspicions, or in any way damages your trust, I wouldn't put up with that.

CERTAINLY, YOU CAN and should have friends of the opposite sex. During my years of counseling, I have come to the conclusion that people with satisfying lives have three to five friends of the same sex and one or two of the opposite sex.

Can you have a friendship with somebody of the opposite sex without it becoming sexual? Absolutely. But if you want to make certain of that, find somebody who is happily engaged in his or her own marital relationship and doesn't have any need for the kind of person that you are. Establish a friendship with somebody of great integrity, somebody who has the ability to make good decisions, somebody who won't become dependent on you.

For instance, I have strong friendships with several women who were former employees of mine. They are great people, are wonderfully married, and are very close friends of mine, and we talk on a regular basis. Those friendships add a great deal to my life. Frankly, that makes my marriage richer and takes some of my sociability load off Marylyn.

If the person you are thinking about marrying regularly exercises poor judgment by getting involved with other people, and it feels to you that this is a risky pattern, listen to your feelings. Don't put up with that without confronting your partner about it. Bring it out on the table and discuss it. Let your partner know your concerns, and if he or she continues the behavior that makes you uneasy, you have reason to question the future of your relationship. On the other hand, if your partner is truly the right person for you, he or she will listen to you and take corrective measures to avoid even the hint of impropriety.

Whatever you do, don't gloss over this area of sociability. If a person is low on sociability, he can get better; sometimes becoming a part of a small group of people is helpful. It would be a mistake, however, to match a highly sociable person with someone who is not. Your desire to be with other people or alone with your partner will be tested again and again in your marriage. It will impact a wide variety of issues, whether it is going out to dinner together with other couples, interacting with and getting involved with people in your community, deciding where you live, or what you will do with your spare time. Make sure that you and your partner are well matched in this area, and the care you take now will be well worth it for years to come.

Qualities That Can Be Developed

SOME OF YOUR personality traits are built in; you didn't have anything to say about whether you'd be an introvert or an extrovert, a bubbly person or more withdrawn. You just woke up one day, and there you were with a full complement of DNA that has forever influenced your life.

But some qualities can be learned if you and your partner will take the time and make the effort. Two of the most important elements in a great marriage fall into this category—adaptability and kindness—and the third dimension in this group, dominance versus submissiveness, is one that will play out every day of your married life. That's why it is so important that you examine these last three areas carefully.

Remember, I've never seen a great marriage in which the couple did not match on at least twenty-five or twenty-six dimensions. If you and your partner are matching well as we go through the dimensions, let your confidence rise about your relationship. But make sure you pay close attention to the crucial qualities of adaptability, kindness, and dominance versus submission. You and your partner want to match well in these areas.

CHAPTER 29

DIMENSION **27** | Adaptability

LONG BEFORE I'D EVER THOUGHT about the twenty-nine dimensions that must be considered in a good relationship, a friend asked me an intriguing question: "If Marylyn ever passed away and you were searching for another mate, what's the number one quality you would look for?"

I thought about my response for a minute or so, then finally answered in one word: "Adaptability."

Now, years later, I'm still convinced that one of the most crucial components to a good relationship is *adaptability*. Indeed, in many ways, it may be the most necessary of all the twenty-nine dimensions. It is the one quality that can make up for problems in some of the other areas. Adaptability is even more important when a couple is not perfectly matched in all twenty-nine dimensions. If a man or a woman can maintain some flexibility, roll with the punches, and adapt to various unforeseen circumstances of life, they have a much better chance of handling the stresses and strains that every marriage is bound to encounter.

Over the life of a marriage, change is inevitable and inexorable. Whether or not we choose it, we will encounter some pretty cataclysmic events in life. How we deal with them can make all the difference in the world. Getting married, having children, dealing with physical health adjustments we must make as we grow older, experiencing the necessary losses of life including the death of a parent or other loved ones—all of these situations create an uneasy pit in the bottom of your stomach and require huge doses of adaptability.

No doubt, adaptability stems from a good, solid self-conception.

Show me a person who is able to adapt to the circumstances life throws at him, and I'll show you somebody whose self-esteem is not tied to what he does, who knows his name, or what he has. He is able to adapt because deep inside he knows he is a person of value, so wherever he is or whatever he does, his life will continue to have intrinsic worth.

If I could give one present to every couple on their wedding day, I'd love to be able to wrap up a large box filled with adaptability. Because no matter how good your relationship is, you will need to be flexible enough to change yourself or at least tolerate your partner's differences. Adaptability may be necessary in matters as mundane as whether you squeeze the toothpaste from the bottom or the top, whether the toilet paper rolls over or under, what time you get out of bed each day—some people prefer to stay up late and get up late, while others want to be in bed by ten and up by six—to where you choose to have your car serviced, to which bank you prefer to handle your accounts. If you are accustomed to doing things one way and your partner has a different habit, one or both of you are going to need a good dose of adaptability.

For instance, April grew up in a home where weekly activities were well coordinated and organized, vacations were planned months in advance, and everyone in the family had a general idea of the schedule.

Sean grew up in a family where plans changed at the drop of a hat. Scheduled doctors' appointments, dinner dates, vacations, or business trips were canceled or changed with little notice. To Sean's family a positive response to an "RSVP" meant merely they were aware of the event and would consider showing up—if nothing else interfered!

When April and Sean struck up a dating relationship, it was only a matter of time before they encountered difficulties over their plans and schedules. Although compatible in many of the twenty-nine dimensions, they were frequently frustrated with each other over scheduling issues. If April planned to do something and Sean chose to change the plan at the last minute, it agitated her. From Sean's perspective, he preferred not to be locked in to a sacrosanct plan; he not only enjoyed being able to change plans at a moment's notice, he prided himself on his ability to do so.

After a few major blowups that nearly cost them their relationship, April and Sean decided to work at adapting to each other in the area of scheduling. It became extremely important that April communicated to Sean what events and plans she considered paramount. "Sean, my friend Rita is getting married on July 7, and I really want to attend the wedding. This is an eight on a scale of one to ten for me."

Sean then took a black ink pen and marked the event on his calendar, knowing that nothing less than a death in the family or nuclear war could change the fact that on July 7 he and April would be attending Rita's wedding.

On April's part, she committed to being more flexible in her schedule for less important matters. "This is a three on my scale of one to ten," she'd tell Sean, "so if we need to do something else, it won't be a big deal." She determined to be more understanding of Sean's desire to keep his schedule open, to take advantage of good opportunities when they came along. The key to April and Sean's ability to get along now and in the future is adaptability, which opens the doors to communication, negotiation, and compromise.

Most of us don't like change. We prefer our comfort zones; the tried and true. But sure enough, just about the time we begin to sit back and relax, something comes along to rock our world.

Joey and Ashley were enjoying life immensely and were getting ready to start a family when, in his early thirties, Joey was transferred to another city by his company. The choice was either to move or seek other employment. Joey and Ashley moved. They moved from a small northern town, where everyone knew their names and their family backgrounds, to a large southern city, where they quickly discovered that "How're y'all doin'" was more of a greeting than a genuine question.

Joey immersed himself in his work, trying to pick up the new systems in the larger office complex, while Ashley attempted to deal with the many details of reestablishing normal life in their new community. She found everything from getting phone and cable television service to finding a quality doctor to be a daunting task. Before long, she began to resent the move, then Joey's job, then, eventually, Joey himself.

Joey was working harder and longer hours than ever before, so by the time he got home from the office, he was physically fatigued and emotionally exhausted. He tried his best to console Ashley, encouraging her that life in their new environment would get better, but he was too drained himself to be much help to her. After a while, he quit trying.

Ashley and Joey soon began to experience trouble in several areas of their relationship. Communication dwindled to perfunctory comments about the weather and Joey's work; their sexual passion dissipated as well. Night after night, they crawled into bed with Joey facing one wall and Ashley facing the other.

Fortunately, Joey and Ashley were well matched in other areas of their relationship, and they were able to recognize the seriousness of what was happening to them. One night after dinner they sat down together, just as tired and frustrated as any other evening, but determined that they were not going to allow their relationship to die as a result of the move.

"We have to make some changes," Joey said.

"I agree, but how?" Ashley asked. "What can we do? Do you want to move back home?"

"No, let's give this move a chance. Let's try to put down some roots in this city, get established somehow, make some new friends, and see how we feel then. If we still think we are not going to fit in here, we'll move back home and I'll find a new job."

Both Joey and Ashley began making an effort to learn more about their new city, its history, the people who lived there, and the recent improvements the city had made to attract newcomers to the area. They went door-to-door in their new neighborhood on a Saturday afternoon to introduce themselves to the neighbors. Most of the neighbors apologized for being so rude in not coming to greet the new residents.

In addition, Joey and Ashley began attending some local churches in their new home city. It was awkward at first, and they were uncomfortable in visiting various congregations, "taste-testing" to see what sort of group met their needs and would provide an opportunity for them to become involved. But before long, they were able to find a church home where they began to connect with people their age, many of whom had also transferred to the area from other places around the country. Beyond that, they found recommendations they could trust for everything from medical help to mundane matters such as trash collection and favorite grocery stores.

As Joey and Ashley continued to adapt to their surroundings instead of complaining about them, their outlook on life improved, as did their personal relationship. Today, Joey and Ashley are living contentedly in their new town, they have two children, and they are on the welcoming committee at their church. But perhaps none of that would have happened had they not had a strong measure of adaptability in their relationship.

Nobody can predict what good things or difficult matters may come to you in marriage, but when you are evaluating the long-term potential of your relationship, both you and your partner having a similar measure of adaptability should be a deciding factor concerning your future together.

CHAPTER 30

DIMENSION **28** | Kindness

IT MIGHT SURPRISE YOU to discover that in survey after survey, both men and women rate kindness as the second most important quality to look for in a mate. Men worldwide, you will recall, most often rate vitality as the number one trait they are looking for in a mate, while women consistently rate security as the number one quality they are looking for in a husband. Both men and women, however, want a mate who is kind.

My dad always said, "Show me someone who is kind to children and older people, and I will show you a trustworthy person." I believe Dad was right. In most cases when somebody consistently extends kindness to someone who does not have the capability or the wherewithal to return the kindness in the same measure, that is a person in whom kindness is a basic part of his or her personality.

Certainly it is possible to display momentary kindness while still having a character disorder, an addiction, an emotional problem, or distorted values. But if a person expresses kindness on a daily basis, you can be relatively sure that a strong vein of goodness runs through that person. When you see the capacity to treat other people with kindness in the everyday actions and reactions of your potential partner, it is a highly encouraging sign.

Watch carefully how your partner treats his or her family members, business associates, friends, or even strangers. Does he rail at other drivers on the highway? Does she cut people off as she is exiting the parking garage, or does she allow people to pull out in front of her? Here again, you can tell a great deal about a person by noting how he or she regards and treats people in service positions—waiters and waitresses, people at toll booths, the girl at the grocery store checkout counter, the person who picks up the trash.

After interviewing prospective new executives for his company, Mr. Jones, a prominent business owner, always invites the interviewee out to breakfast at a busy diner-type restaurant. The potential executive usually strides to the table with a great deal of confidence. After all, he's been invited to have breakfast with the man who owns the company! But on more than a few occasions, the executive has been sent packing, back to job hunting following the breakfast. Why? Because he didn't do well in an interview? No. Because he was incompetent for the position? No. He was not hired because of the way he disrespected, disregarded, or otherwise mistreated the waitress.

"If he will be rude or inconsiderate to the man or woman bringing his breakfast," noted Mr. Jones, "he will not be concerned for our employees under his supervision. It is a facet of his character. On the other hand, if he is kind and cordial to people who have no capacity to do anything for him, respecting them, treating them with dignity, assuming all of his other managerial skills are adequate, he will usually be a good manager of our people."

Look for such subtle evidences of kindness in the person with whom you are considering spending the rest of your life. Don't be fooled by initial gestures of kindness on the part of your partner. Most people are usually kind to one another when they first begin dating. Just because he sends you a beautiful arrangement of flowers does not mean he is a kind person; he may just know a good florist. The fact that she buys you a special present early in your relationship may show that she was thinking about you, but it does not necessarily imply that she will reciprocate your kindness over time.

Observe acts and attitudes of kindness in the little things. Watch for him to open the car door for you; does she thank you when you bring in the mail for her? Does he offer unsolicited compliments on your new sweater or blouse? Does she encourage you to do your best and not to be discouraged when things don't work out the way you had planned? Are basic acts and words of consideration, such as "please," "thank you," and "no, thank you" a regular part of your partner's conversation? When you and your partner treat each other with this sort of kindness, it will enrich your relationship, whether you eventually marry or not.

Kevin and Susan have been dating for nearly a year, and the kindness in their relationship seems to be extremely one-sided. It seems that Susan is constantly complimenting him on his appearance and his abilities, applauding him for his achievements, touting his athletic prowess, doing kind things for Kevin, helping him with his workload, typing papers for him, running errands, and buying presents for his children from a previous marriage. Susan doesn't think her expressions of kindness are anything extraordinary and, apparently, neither does Kevin. He hardly ever thanks her for the many things she does for him.

The truly great marriages are those in which both partners express, reciprocate, and appreciate kindness. He holds the chair for her as she is seated in a restaurant. She picks up his laundry without being asked. He constantly tells her how attractive she is to him; she lets him know that she is attracted to him as well. He helps her unload the groceries or her suitcases from the car. She freely expresses genuine admiration for his strength of character and intelligence. He appreciates her ability to compete and succeed in the workplace. She gets up early on Saturday morning to accompany him to the airport, when he could just as easily drive himself. It almost seems they are trying to outdo each other in their expressions of kindness toward each other. Ironically, if you were to point out these deeds, words, and attitudes to the individuals, they would be surprised that anyone noticed their acts of kindness. They simply enjoy treating one another kindly.

When you are considering a person as a possible marriage partner, make sure he or she is a kind person. And while you are at it, be sure that the person whose face you see in your mirror is a kind person as well.

CHAPTER 31

DIMENSION **29** | # Dominance Versus Submissiveness

A DOMINANT PERSONALITY is the person who always wants to be the boss; he wants to decide where to eat dinner tonight; she wants absolute say on what color the drapes should be in your home. The dominant person doesn't always mean to be the first one to speak up, the one with the strongest opinions, loudest complaint, or most vociferous case for what needs to be done—he just is.

In contrast, the submissive person acquiesces willingly when the slightest pressure is exerted or opposition is raised against him or her. She is a peacemaker, does not like to fight, and would rather be taken advantage of than oppose anything but the most glaring inequity.

Oddly enough, in marriage the relationship will often work better if one person is somewhat dominant and the other is slightly submissive. It doesn't seem to matter whether the dominant person is male or female, as long as they are not both bucking for power and authority. Our research shows that when both partners are high in dominance, they will eventually go to war with each other. When both partners are high in submissiveness, they will eventually go to sleep on each other. They will bore each other to death!

You probably don't want to marry someone who is extremely dominant, even if you are extremely submissive. That usually does not work well in marriage. Nor should two submissive people be paired together.

In the best marriages, the individuals will both have moderate amounts of dominance and submissiveness. For example, Marylyn can be very dominant in some areas, and I'm happy she is. By the same token, I can be rather dominant regarding some matters, and she may be more submissive in those areas. It is not a matter of one person being king and the other being the servant; it is a matter of working together for the best in the relationship. In a good relationship, the individuals have a little fire, but they also have a lot of unselfishness.

"I hate that restaurant!" I'll object to Marylyn. "But do you really want to go there?"

"Yes, I do."

"Why do you want to go there?"

"Because they have that great soup!"

"Oh, yes; you're right. They do. Let's go to that restaurant!"

In that case, I started out being extremely dominant, and ended up being quite submissive. I don't think Marylyn would like me a great deal if I just said, "Well, honey, where would you like to go? I'll just go wherever you want to go" and rolled over and played dead every time she made a suggestion. Nor would I want to be the absolute dictator of our relationship.

Indecisiveness is one of the most irritating aspects of the submissive person's make up; totalitarianism can be one of the most dangerous aspects of the person who is high in dominance. Ideally, a good relationship will have a balance of both.

HAVING LOOKED AT all twenty-nine dimensions that must be considered in a great marriage, you can now better understand this statement: *If anybody has a behavioral or personality issue that you are not willing to live with for a lifetime, don't marry that person!* Before you pledge yourself to another person for life, you must know yourself extremely well. You should also know your partner extremely well, which is why at eHarmony we recommend that couples be together for at least two years before getting married. Obviously, many couples who are matched on eHarmony feel they are so well matched they want to speed up the process, and many do. But we nonetheless encourage couples to take their time and know each other well. It's also important to have a good grip on your willpower, because over the years you will experience many challenges even in the best of relationships. If you or your partner does not remain the same, you must be able to call upon your willpower to continue honoring the commitment you have made in marriage.

Which of the twenty-nine dimensions are most important? They all are crucial, but if you want to prioritize them, the top two would have to be emotional health and character issues. Give yourself a person who tells the truth and lives it out, and has dealt with all the "emotional junk" in his or her life, and you will significantly increase your odds of having a successful marriage. No marriage can survive without emotional health and good character. If a marriage is not built on these foundational pillars, the individuals will have to continually build, rebuild, patch, scrape, and clean, and that marriage will eventually grow tired. And when you get weary in well doing, you are open to every kind of aspirant—drugs, alcohol, an affair, a hobby that gets in the way of the marriage, or a host of other negative factors.

Avoid that mess. Don't settle for anyone who has less than the best emotional health and character.

Moreover, in analyzing your relationship in light of the twenty-nine dimensions, look for a lot of similarities. As we've noted numerous times, it is not how high or low you score on a particular quality, but whether you and your partner are well matched in those areas. Finding someone who is a lot like you will make the difference down the road (more about that in the next chapter), and if you don't find a preponderance of similarities between you and your partner, you must reevaluate your relationship.

People often ask me, "Neil, how well do you and Marylyn stack up on the twenty-nine dimensions? Are you matched well in every area?"

Often I see a look of surprise show on their faces when I reply, "No, we are not."

Do we match on intellect? Yes.

Do we have similar energy levels? Yes.

Are we compatible in the area of spirituality? Absolutely.

We could go down the list, and in almost every area, Marylyn and I are a good match. I mentioned previously that we don't always see political issues from the same perspective, but that would never be a wedge between us, because we have so many other strong points in our marriage. But it could be a major factor for a couple who were not strongly matched in other areas. I must confess that I have never seen a great marriage in which the couple were not matched on at least twenty-five or twenty-six of the twenty-nine dimensions.

When you've cleansed the junk out of your relationship, and you've found a person with whom you have a large number of similarities, then look at the issues of kindness and adaptability. Are you treating each other kindly? Do you communicate well with each other?

Of course, there is one more factor that you must consider. If the twenty-nine dimensions are the engine on which your marriage will travel long-term, *chemistry* is the key that will crank your motor and keep it going. Let's look at this essential key that you and your partner must possess before you embark on the lifelong journey of marriage.

CHAPTER 32

Chemistry— The Key Factor

HANNAH THOMPSON grew up in a small town in Kansas; Steve Sloan grew up in a town a short distance away, yet he and Hannah never met.

A bright, beautiful, outgoing young woman, Hannah graduated from high school and enrolled at a well-known southwestern university. Handsome, ambitious, and intelligent, Steve, too, decided to attend . . . you guessed it . . . the same university. The two attractive young people completed college, living on campus most of that time— and still they never met!

"I was aware of Steve," Hannah said later. "I'd heard his name, but I had no idea what he looked like."

Upon graduation, Hannah took a position with Mercy Ministries of America, an organization working with "at risk" young women. Hannah moved to the location of the organization's headquarters in Nashville. Steve moved to Nashville as well and began a video production company along with some friends. He and Hannah still had not met.

Meanwhile, unbeknownst to the other person, both Hannah and Steve had signed on to eHarmony. About that same time, a friend of Hannah's contacted her to tell her about a guy who had moved to Nashville and was looking for a good church. Would Hannah be willing to invite him to church, strictly as a gesture of friendship?

Hannah's outgoing, friendly personality could handle that easily. When she contacted the fellow concerning the church service, she discovered that it was Steve. They went to church together, enjoyed the service, and then parted ways.

One day Steve's company received a phone call from Mercy Ministries concerning the possibility of working on a project for the ministry. As the marketing director of the organization, Hannah was soon talking to Steve by phone on a regular basis.

A few days went by, and Hannah received a match notice from eHarmony: "Steve from Nashville would like to communicate with you." When Hannah examined the profile of "Steve from Nashville," she was amazed. "I think I know this guy," she said. The more she compared the profile to her recall of Steve, the more convinced she was that they were one and the same.

The next time Steve called regarding the video production, Hannah boldly asked, "Steve, are you on eHarmony?"

The phone went silent for a long moment. "Why do you ask?" he finally managed to say.

Hannah smiled. "You may want to check your eHarmony account," she said. "I think you will find a very interesting match there."

Sure enough, when Steve checked his account, Hannah's photograph was on his computer screen. They were a match. Although they had lived in the same vicinity, in three separate states, over a lifetime, they had never met until a few days previously, and now they discovered that they shared an enormous amount of compatibility.

With all that going for them, you might assume that Steve and Hannah couldn't book a wedding planner fast enough. Not so.

The couple was missing one crucial ingredient necessary of soul mates—they lacked chemistry. Consequently, they wisely limited their relationship to being friends.

If you and your partner match well on all twenty-nine dimensions, have you discovered your soul mate? Not exactly. You've found one person who might qualify as a soul mate for you. You may have merely found a good friend who is a lot like you. One other factor must be considered if you are searching for your soul mate. In some ways, it is the most difficult factor of all, since it is so ambiguous. That is the area of *chemistry*. With some people you simply click, and with others you don't.

At eHarmony, we have been studying chemistry for some time, trying to better define what it is and how you can tell when you have it with another person. We have found that there are certain physiological responses that take place in your body when you meet a person with whom you have chemistry; the pupils in your eyes enlarge, your skin temperature warms, and a myriad of other things happen in your body when you are in the presence of someone with whom you have good chemistry. Many of these responses lead to sexual passion, but why those responses are evoked and what characteristics elicit them can be different in every person. Frankly, trying to define chemistry is like trying to nail fog to the wall.

But if you are looking for your soul mate, you must match well on nearly all the twenty-nine dimensions and then find the person with that curiously indefinable quality known as chemistry. We've had people on our eHarmony site for whom we have provided many good, solid matches, people that we know scientifically are compatible with them. But when they pursued getting to know the person with whom they were matched, nothing clicked. There was no fire. For some people, we have provided several hundred matches before they ever found their soul mate. That's okay. We encourage them not to marry someone if the chemistry is not right.

Love Minus Chemistry Equals Friendship

Without chemistry, you do not have a soul mate; you have a good friend. I once wrote an article for a magazine talking about the importance of chemistry in a relationship. I made a strong statement: "Don't ever marry anybody with whom you don't have a lot of chemistry."

Some people say, "I don't feel very turned on by him or her, but I think we should go ahead and get married and we will develop a passion for each other. Don't you agree?" I always say, "No, I don't agree. If you don't feel turned on by the other person, hold on. That may be a clear sign that you are not compatible."

In the article I discussed the physical aspects of chemistry, wanting to hold hands with the person to whom you are attracted, wanting to touch, to hug. I wrote about the desire to kiss the other person and being physically drawn to the other person.

I hadn't given the article a title, so the magazine entitled it "Love Minus Chemistry Equals Friendship."

I said, "Wow, that is dead-on." If you have somebody that you care for a lot, but you don't have any chemistry with him or her, don't even think about marrying that person. It just isn't possible to make a marriage work well if you are not drawn to the other person physically.

Some people say, "I want to fall in love with my best friend. I want to be friends before we fall in love, before the chemistry becomes a part of it." That makes a lot of sense, and I'd encourage you to develop dating relationships with someone you like as a friend. Often the best marriage partners are best friends. Having somebody that you trust and like and want to be around is a great start for a couple trying to figure out whether or not they can have a lifetime together. If they have a good friendship, that is an important plus. But if that is indeed all they have, if after a while they do not have any chemistry, they should keep the relationship platonic and enjoy it. They should not expect it to develop further, nor would it necessarily be wise to allow it to do so.

Often when I try to define *chemistry*, I fall back on a story from my own life. Early one morning I was reading my favorite newspaper comic strip, "Calvin and Hobbes," drawn and written by Bill Waterson. I was about to write the book *Finding the Love of Your Life*, and I was grappling with how to describe what it means to fall in love. That's when I found a particularly insightful edition of "Calvin and Hobbes."

If you were never privileged to see the strip before Bill Waterson retired, you should understand that Calvin is a little boy, and Hobbes is a stuffed tiger that comes alive when Calvin is alone with it. Hobbes has a personality all his own.

In the strip that caught my eye, Calvin looks at Hobbes and asks, "What is it like to fall in love?"

Hobbes stops walking, looks into space, strokes his chin, and says, "Well, say the object of your affection walks by."

"Yeah?" says Calvin, looking up at his friend expectantly.

"First, your heart falls into your stomach and splashes your innards," Hobbes says, swinging his hand around to demonstrate someone who is sweating profusely, and wiping his forehead. "This condensation shorts the circuits to your brain, and you get all woozy. When your brain burns out altogether, your mouth disengages, and you babble like a cretin until she leaves."

"That's love?" Calvin asks, obviously shocked.

"Medically speaking," Hobbes intones, clearly taken with his description.

Calvin concludes, "That happened to me once, and I figured it was cooties!"

From a psychological standpoint, Waterson got it pretty accurate. First, your heart falls into your stomach and splashes your innards. That is chemistry! When you see that person and something inside you just goes crazy, that is chemistry.

I still recall when, as a senior at Pepperdine University, I walked into the Oasis one day, the campus grille, and there was a cute freshman girl. I was so taken with her. I wore glasses at the time, so I took my glasses off and inconspicuously slipped them inside my sweater and into my shirt pocket.

The only problem was that I was so enamored with the pretty young freshman woman and so jittery in trying to make a first impression on her, that I missed my shirt pocket, and the glasses slid all the way down my stomach, out the bottom of my sweater, and shattered all over the floor. That's what chemistry can do to you; all the nerve endings in your body are just jangled, creating a nerve-racking, wonderful, frightening, sweet sensation.

There is no reasoning involved; this is chemical by nature. But be careful. While love without chemistry equals friendship, chemistry alone is not a foundational building block of your relationship. It is the icing, not the cake. If all you have is chemistry, that is not enough. Somebody said, "Passion, though a bad regulator, is a good spring." In other words, it is good at getting love going, but not so good at keeping it going. The chemistry of passion, without a base of deeper, more important compatibilities, typically lasts only about six to eight months. If you proceed to marriage on that basis alone and move too quickly, you will get yourself into a lot of trouble. But if you get into a relationship and you don't have a lot of passion, be careful.

Chemistry is the indispensable agent in your relationship; it is the glue that will hold a couple together through the hard times as well as bringing great joy to their relationship during the good times. Don't leave for your wedding without it.

CHAPTER 33

Commitment—
The Glue That
Keeps It All Together

CAN YOU EVER REALLY know a person well enough to make an unconditional commitment of your life to him or her?

Yes, I believe you can. In fact, that unconditional type of commitment is the only environment that will truly allow a marriage to flourish. It is a commitment that holds a couple together during those difficult periods that come to every marriage—during the first few years, during the "flat" places, when boredom or routine sets in, as well as times when the relationship hits a snag and you or your partner wants to walk out the door and not come back. Commitment may not completely alleviate the concern that your partner will pack up and leave, but it significantly eases those fears of abandonment. You have made a public promise declaring that you will stick with each other through thick and thin. That promise alone carries incredible power.

Perhaps the most important benefit of commitment is that it allows trust and intimacy to develop in your relationship, even during the times when the two of you may not be at your best. If you know deep down that you and your partner are committed to each other, that you will not leave the relationship, you can have incredible confidence to address things that need to be improved, while providing a security that "live-in lovers" can never know.

But the time to think about commitment is now, before you make it! Consider carefully what it means when you say, "I love you; I want to marry you; I am committing the remainder of my life to you." If you cannot make a full, unreserved commitment to your partner, don't get married. Even if you meet on eHarmony and know that you are a perfect match, I still encourage you to take your time. In that regard, allow me to offer seven cautions that could possibly prevent you from making a mistake.

Seven Checkpoints Before You Say, "I Do"

1. *Take plenty of time to evaluate your relationship* before deciding to get married. Even for those couples who are excellently matched, I suggest that you date for one to two years. During the first year, most people are still on their best behavior. You don't usually encounter too many problems that test the quality of your relationship until the second year. Allow yourself enough time to see your potential partner under stress and in difficult times, as well as idealistic, good times.

"One or two years!" Betty protested when I suggested that she continue dating Dwayne longer than the few months they had known each other before talking about marriage. "Dr. Warren, I am forty-three years old. I have been married once before. If I wait two more years, I'll be ancient!"

Well, not exactly. But regardless of age or prior "experience," research shows that couples who take one to two years or more getting to know each other consistently have a much higher level of marital satisfaction.

2. *Make sure you are the right age to get married.* This, of course, is a concern for younger couples, especially those in their early twenties. The truth is, the divorce rate for twenty-one-year-olds is twice that of twenty-five-year-olds. Too often when a person marries extremely young, he doesn't really know who he is yet; he doesn't know what he truly wants out of life, let alone what sort of partner he needs. You can give yourself a tremendous head start in marriage if you wait until you and your partner are at least in your mid-twenties.

3. *Beware of being overeager.* Some people are so eager to get married that they ignore the facts of the relationship. Remember, if your partner displays any of the seven screening dimensions, slow down, stop, look, and listen. You may need to leave that relationship; regardless, take another look, and make sure you know what you are getting into. Other people view marriage as an escape hatch, the door to getting them out of a bad situation, the answer to their loneliness or financial difficulties. Inevitably, if someone gets married for such wrong reasons, the relationship will crumble. The foundation is simply not strong enough to support it. Make sure that you are marrying for all the right reasons.

4. *Make yourself happy.* As we've said previously, don't get married to make anyone else happy; the one person you must please in your mate selection is yourself. Take advice from your parents, peers, friends, and wise counselors but, ultimately, if you get married to please anyone else—even your partner—you will be committing yourself to a lifetime of regrets.

5. *Make sure you have a broad spectrum of experiences* before committing to marriage. Many couples have an extremely narrow base of dating experiences. Perhaps they see each other only at church or at school, or within certain groups, such as a softball league, a writers group, or at dance parties.

Others engage in long-distance relationships that provide only a minimum of "real-life" experiences. I've even heard of people who have gotten married to men or women while they were in prison! It is impossible to truly know a person with whom you have such limited contact.

Still other couples have simply not experienced enough of life together to make an intelligent appraisal of their potential future. They are "in love," and that's all that matters to them. I liken them to an airplane approaching a beautiful mass of fluffy, white, billowy clouds. Everything looks good as the plane zooms through the sky—but behind the clouds stands a huge mountain!

To make sure you have the right person for marriage, broaden your experiences to see your potential mate in as many different circumstances as possible—in good times and tough times, important matters or mundane.

6. *Make sure your expectations are realistic.* Often our expectations of marriage relate directly to what we've seen modeled for us by our parents. But as we've noted, many times our parents' relationships were not the best, either. Sometimes just the opposite is true, that our parents made marriage look too easy! The truth of the matter is that every good marriage takes work. Get a grip on what real life is going to be like with your partner before you decide to get married.

7. *Address any character issues, behavioral problems, or personality quirks before getting married.* As we mentioned earlier, any character disorders that you discover in yourself or your partner ought to delay your trip down the wedding aisle. Likewise, red flags such as jealousy, irresponsibility, or stubbornness are often ingrained in a person. They don't go away merely with time, nor do they improve automatically. If you have any doubts about your ability or willingness to make an irrevocable commitment to your partner, or you question your partner's ability to make such a commitment to you, slow down! You will not lose anything by taking more time to check things out; you could lose a lot if you plunge into marriage with any danger signs flashing.

Vows? What Vows?

In ancient cultures, public vows exchanged between individuals could rarely be broken outside death. Nowadays, we tend to be much more lenient, often giving the impression that commitment is to be taken seriously only when it is convenient or pleasant. Nothing could be farther from the truth, especially in regard to the marriage commitment. If you really want to get married, you should understand what you are signing up for.

To do so, let's take a look at the traditional marriage vows.

Granted, many modern marriages use various forms of these vows, and some couples write their own. But if the relationship is to be a true marriage, two individuals will make some serious promises to each other. The minister or other legally accountable person who is conducting the wedding will ask something like this:

> Neil, do you take Marylyn to be your wife, and do you solemnly promise to love, honor, and cherish her, and that forsaking all others for her alone, you will perform unto her all the duties that a husband owes to his wife until God by death shall separate you?

If I answer affirmatively, the minister will lead me in the marriage vows:

> I, Neil, take you, Marylyn, to be my wife. I promise and covenant before God and these witnesses to be your loving and faithful husband—in plenty and in want, in joy and in sorrow, in sickness and in health—as long as we both shall live.

Most people watching the wedding are hoping that the two people taking the vows will stay in the marriage, that they will not get a divorce or otherwise leave the relationship. Yet we know that approximately 75 percent of marriages end unhappily. A few years later, if you ask many marriage partners, "Why are you staying in this marriage? You are not happy in it. Why are you still there?" they have various reasons.

Some of them say, "Well, you know I pledged myself for a lifetime."

"You pledged yourself to what?"

"I pledged myself to stay in the marriage."

"Oh, really? Is that what you did?"

"Yeah, that's what I did. We're not getting along too well, and we're not having much fun, but I committed myself to hang in there, to put up with the old ball and chain, so that's what I'm doing."

Other people will say, "I am staying in the marriage because of my kids. I don't want my kids living in that bifurcated world of divorce."

Still others will say, "Well, I need to stay with him because I have strong religious beliefs," or "My parents have such deep convictions about marriage. They'd practically die if I got a divorce."

But is that really what the marriage vows mean? I'm convinced that I committed to do much more than merely remain in the marriage. I see at least six specific vows that I made to Marylyn on our wedding day.

Six Promises and Bonds of Commitment

1. LOVE   Notice the way the first question is asked: "Neil, do you solemnly promise to love Marylyn?"

It is not always easy to love someone. Sometimes it's even tougher to *like* your partner! Frequently, I will ask somebody, "Do you like your wife?"

And they say, "Why, of course."

"No, I don't mean do you love your wife; do you like her?" In marriage, you promise to love your spouse, even on days when you don't like her very much, when you disagree over something or simply feel badly. When you love somebody, you can sometimes look over some things that aren't so pleasurable and say, "I love you in spite of those things." Love means that you do not withdraw any worth or value from the other person, regardless of how you feel. At times, you may think, *I don't like you too much right now, but I still regard you as a person of great worth and value.* That's what unconditional love is all about.

2. HONOR   The second question is: "Neil, do you solemnly promise to love and *honor* Marylyn?" When you honor someone, you treat them with respect even when they are different from you. You honor them with your words, with your eye contact, with your attention, and your actions. You are basically saying, "You are important to me."

3. CHERISH   Next you hear, "Do you solemnly promise to love, honor, and *cherish* your partner?"

Lady Bird Johnson, wife of former president Lyndon B. Johnson, used to say to her daughters whenever they left her presence, "You are cherished." I have always liked that. To cherish someone is to treat them with tender affection. In the marriage vows, you promise to have that kind of tender, cherishing affection for your partner even under circumstances that aren't necessarily easy or pleasant. That is a big promise. It requires self-sacrifice; it means setting aside your own desires and needs at that moment so you might better meet the needs of your spouse.

4. FORSAKE ALL OTHERS   The fourth part of the vows says I will *forsake all others* for her alone. That is not merely forsaking all others sexually, although that is certainly implied in the vow. I believe it means you will have a loyalty to him or to her. You will make your partner your top priority. You forsake all others. From the day you say, "I do," your partner is the human being who is the most important person in your life. You do not play around with competitive voices calling to you from outside the marriage or compromising impulses within you. Your partner can have deep and total trust in you because you have forsaken all others for her alone.

5. PERFORM ALL DUTIES   Number five is particularly interesting: It says that a husband will perform unto his spouse all the duties that a husband owes to his wife. What duties does a husband owe to his wife? Certainly a husband will protect his wife physically to the best of his ability. Equally important is protecting her emotionally. He won't let a brother, sister, mother, father, or anyone else say or do anything to insult, harass, cajole, ridicule, or damage his wife emotionally.

If you are a woman, you have a responsibility to be extremely protective of your husband as well. You will make sure to the best of your ability that he is well nurtured, not only in terms of food and rest, but also in terms of his emotional life. Certainly, part of that commitment involves being sexually available to one another on a reasonable frequency—that a wife will perform to her husband all the duties a wife owes to her husband, and that a husband will perform unto his wife all the duties a husband owes to his wife.

6. UNDER EVERY KIND OF CIRCUMSTANCE; AS LONG AS WE BOTH SHALL LIVE   The sixth portion of the vows may be the most difficult of all—that you will do the first five *under every kind of circumstance*. In plenty and in want, in joy and in sorrow, in sickness and in health, *as long as we both shall live*.

That includes when you are tired, stressed, or when you are physically sick. Think about that when she comes home with all those packages she purchased using that brand-new credit card. Think about that when he leaves his dirty clothes on the floor for the umpteenth time after you've told him the dirty laundry goes in the hamper. You have already promised to love, honor, cherish her, and forsake all others for her love, and perform to her all the duties a husband owes to his wife, under all kinds of circumstances, for as long as the two of you live!

During the summer of 2004, the world watched in awe as the United States grieved the death of and paid tribute to President Ronald Reagan. Many accolades were heaped on the late president as leaders from around the world repeatedly drew attention to his boldness, his sense of humor, and his integrity. Again and again, however, admirers acknowledged the true source of his strength—the unconditional love of his wife, Nancy. Mrs. Reagan's commitment to her husband was all the more impressive in that she continued to honor and respect him to the day he died, nearly a decade after he had lost his full ability to reciprocate her love due to a prolonged, debilitating case of Alzheimer's disease. Nancy Reagan's love for Ronald Reagan was certainly not "I will love for as long as it is convenient." Nor was it "I will love as long as you can meet my needs." Nancy Reagan's love for her husband was a picture of unconditional love as reflected in the marriage vows she took so many years earlier.

Although the words of the marriage vows may change over time, the commitment will always remain serious and all-encompassing. If you are not prepared to make this kind of lifelong pledge to your partner, you are not ready to be married. That doesn't make you less of a person; in fact, it may show signs of maturity and wisdom if you realize that you are not ready for the commitment of marriage and refuse to consider it until you are.

The problem, of course, is that the culture in which we live has never figured out how to get the marital relationship off to the right start. For the most part, society doesn't have the first idea how to match people for broad-based compatibility. Consequently, the culture builds in "escape hatches" to marriage that the relationship was never intended to have. We have been so concerned about not trapping people in a relationship in which they are mismatched that we have flung open the doors to divorce court, giving the impression that commitment in marriage is a colossal joke, a broken legal contract, a mess that must be cleaned up, or nothing more than a failed business deal.

The Good News

We now know how to help people get well matched, so well matched that they can remain married for the long term, through good times and bad times. What we want couples to say is, "Even though times get hard, I will not leave this marriage."

Now, that makes sense only if the individuals are well matched in the beginning, and if they have all the characteristics we know are important for a long lasting relationship. That is what is so exciting about eHarmony to me; with our matching model, we can bring together two people who have the potential for lifelong love and happiness. That doesn't necessarily make commitment easy. I would never want to imply that you can simply go down through our checklist for a good relationship and life will be all honey and no bees. But I am confident we can provide you with the tools and enough information to change the odds in your favor to find the person with whom you can confidently share that kind of commitment.

Throughout this book, I have repeatedly advised that if you are not well matched with your partner, now is the time to exit the relationship. Don't continue the relationship out of convenience, laziness, or concern for other people's opinions. When there are significant problems in a dating relationship, nine times out of ten they don't get better. Save yourself and your partner a lot of pain and heartache, and kindly tell each other the truth. Remember to put any potentially hurtful truth into a good context that maintains your dignity and that of your partner. Up until you say the words "I do," you still have the option of walking away from the relationship if you are not totally sure you are well matched.

Once the marriage vows are taken, however, once you and another person have pledged yourselves to each other for a lifetime, you have every responsibility to make that relationship work. With a few puffs of air, your entire focus changes; you are linked to another person for life. Your goal now is to make that marriage one in which you love, honor, and cherish your mate for a lifetime. You and your partner can do that when you fall in love for all the right reasons!

Just the other day I was in my office looking at some photographs of couples who would be joining me in the filming of a new television commercial for eHarmony that would be broadcast all across the U.S. and in many parts of the world. I smiled as I recalled the first couple who notified us that they were planning to get married after having been matched on eHarmony. I'm not sure who was more excited—the engaged couple or our fledgling staff at eHarmony. "It works! It works!" we said, almost to our surprise.

He was from Salem, Oregon, and she was from San Antonio, Texas. He was one of the first men to sign on to our site, and was willing to travel anywhere to find the right woman. She, on the other hand, had been encouraged to get on the site by her mom, and she preferred someone within thirty miles of her home. They were matched by our system, but she was a bit reticent. "I really wanted someone from around San Antonio," she confessed to him. "How did I get you?"

"If you turn out to be the woman I think you are," he said, "I will *be* within thirty miles of your home, in San Antonio, or wherever you need me to be!"

Soon the stories of successful matches began rolling in, and every story was pure gold to us. Each one brought tears to our eyes. It worked again! We're up to four marriages. Five, six, seven! Soon we heard about the first baby being born to a couple that we matched on eHarmony. To think that we were now influencing the next generation was something we had only dreamed about. Now, it was happening.

Today, we know it works.

So, if you find a person with whom you have broad-based compatibility, you can be assured that your relationship will have what it takes to last a lifetime. The twenty-nine key dimensions I have described in this book have helped thousands of people find their soul mates and fall in love for all the right reasons. I am deeply confident these truths will work for you too!

Three Secrets
to a Great Relationship

IN THIS BOOK, much of our discussion has been about evaluating your potential partner in marriage. But if you want to find your soul mate and fall in love for all the right reasons, you must also discover three essential things about yourself:

1. It is important to know clearly who you are.
2. It is important to know clearly the similarities in a partner that are important to you.
3. Finally, you should be aware of those traits you must have and those you can't stand in a relationship.

Let's look at these three elements individually.

Know Yourself

You now know that to have a great marriage, you must match your partner in as many of the twenty-nine dimensions as possible. But to match someone else in the twenty-nine dimensions, you must also know who you are in regard to those matters. To help do that, you need to get a clear idea of the people, events, and influences that have helped shape you into the person you are today. Most single people are overwhelmed with this idea at first. They say, "How in the world can I figure out who I am? Am I supposed to go off by myself to the desert or to the mountains and meditate on the great issues of life?"

That may not be necessary, although going away for a weekend re-treat someplace where you can spend some time alone, away from televisions, telephones, e-mails, and other distractions could be time well spent. Regardless where you go or don't go, there are five prac-tical things I recommend to help you better know yourself.

1. PLAY TWENTY QUESTIONS   I've developed twenty questions to help you get a handle on the people and events that have had a pro-found impact on you and have helped make you into the unique per-son you are. I encourage you to write a short paragraph in response to these questions (to find the complete list, refer to Appendix B in the back of this book). The questions range from "Who is the most important person in your life, and why?" to "What is the one dream for your life you most look forward to achieving?" to "What specifi-cally would you like your closest friends to say about you at your funeral?"

By the time you carefully answer all twenty questions, you will be amazed at what a clear picture you will have of yourself. It is crucial for you to figure out who you are before you go shopping for some-body with whom you want to live the rest of your life. Moreover, it is imperative that you have this picture in mind, because that is the per-son your soul mate is searching for.

2. DISCUSS YOUR ANSWERS   We've already acknowledged that other people can sometimes see certain things about us more clearly than we can (or want to) see for ourselves. Their insights about you may cause you to seek a soul mate slightly different from the person you had in mind. To take advantage of this information, ask two or three close friends or family members to read your responses to the twenty questions. Say something such as, "Do you think I'm shooting straight with myself?"

"Oh, I can do the first part," I hear you fretting, "but to take my re-sponses to some friends or family members might be too embarrass-ing or too personal. They might not want to help me out."

Possibly not, but give it a try. Simply say to your friend or family member, "Would you please read this? You may have some understandings or insights into me that I don't have. I don't want to be blind to things about myself, so I want your brutally honest feedback to these answers. Tell me if you think I have a pretty good view of myself, or if there are any areas where you think I'm off target."

3. DRAW YOUR FAMILY TREE   Draw a rough sketch of your family tree, placing each name in a circle on a branch. Jot down some notes about each person for whom you can find any information, and in particular how the information relates to you. For instance, what were your ancestors like? Where did they come from; where did they settle originally? How are you similar to them? Choose two or three of your relatives who have had the most profound impact on you and expand your notes about them to a paragraph or more; chances are your identity is similar to theirs. Most of us nowadays can trace our lineage back only a generation or two, to our grandparents or great grandparents. If you dig into some family photo albums or historical documents, you may be able to glean even more information.

Look at your family heritage and you will begin to recognize how your attitudes, understandings, and values about life developed. As you notice themes, you begin to see patterns in those relationships, and you can see where both the good and the bad have been passed down from one generation to the next. All of these things have contributed either positively or negatively to the person you are today.

4. REVIEW YOUR HISTORY IN FIVE-YEAR SEGMENTS   The person you are today is made up of the person you have been during the various periods of your life. You are not unconnected to the person you were at five years of age, or ten, or fifteen, or twenty, even though you may be a very different person now than you were at each of those phases of your life. But all of those persons are part of who you are today. To understand the person you are today, it greatly helps to understand the person you were at five, ten, or fifteen.

In my seminars I encourage audience members to actually engage in conversations with themselves at various ages of their lives. I tell them, "Just imagine you are walking down a country road, when you meet yourself as a five-year-old. What would that five-year-old talk to you about?" I then instruct the adults to tell that child what they appreciate about him or her, and I ask the "child" to tell the adult what it was like being that person during that time. We then do the same for the child at ten years of age, fifteen, twenty, and twenty-five.

The insights that can be uncovered about yourself through this process are absolutely astounding.

5. TAKE ONE OR MORE PSYCHOLOGICAL INVENTORIES   It is easier than ever to take a personality questionnaire, especially now that eHarmony exists. You can get on the eHarmony.com site, and if you simply want to receive your personality profile, you can do so. Admittedly, it is 436 questions, and it takes more than an hour to complete the test, but you will learn an immense amount of information about who you are. You can become an expert on the subject of you!

Of course, there are all sorts of psychological tests available for you to take nowadays (although many must be administered by a professional counselor), and each of these instruments is designed to tell you something significant about yourself. The more you know about yourself, the better prepared you will be to find your soul mate.

Look for Someone a Lot Like You

Dissimilarities create the need for negotiation; negotiation almost always creates the need for compromise, and compromise will always require you to stretch or bend, which causes tension and is not always easy to handle. Even if you do make the necessary changes, you will still experience the stress and strain that accompany change. Let's be honest; there is enough change in the best of relationships even when you have a lot of things in common. Why ask for more change if you can possibly avoid the hassles by finding a partner who is more like you?

When you don't have a lot of similarities, marriage becomes a struggle. Both of you begin to feel isolated and alone. The person you are living and sleeping with becomes a stranger, and those areas of dissimilarity seem to expand, creating hurt, frustration, and anger.

People often ask me, "How many similarities do you need to have a great relationship?" Or, to put it another way, "Is it all right to have some dissimilarities?"

Yes, it is okay to have a few areas in which you and your mate are radically different, but not many. In the book *Finding the Love of Your Life*, I included a fifty-item list of helpful marriage similarities. The list, which can be found on the eHarmony Web site, includes such matters as:

- Expected roles for both persons within the marriage
- Desire for verbal intimacy and ability to be intimate
- Hobbies and interests
- Attitudes about cleanliness—house, clothes, body, etc.
- Size and style of house
- How to spend vacations
- Temperature of the home during the day and night

When two individuals' attitudes are similar toward these matters and many more, it makes for a more stable and satisfying marriage.

"How many of these fifty do we need to have in common?" someone asks. "All fifty?"

"No, you don't want to marry your clone," I tell them. On the other hand, I like couples to have their similarities in the high thirties or low forties out of our list of fifty. You don't want to have too many things that you fuss about. For instance, a couple gets together and he likes to watch action movies or sports on television, and she likes to watch drama and the arts. She likes to go to bed early, and he likes to go to bed late. She likes to get up early; he likes to get up late. He is really excited about sex, and she is not as interested in sex. She is a very spiritual person and wants to attend church or synagogue on the weekends. He is not into religion and wants to play golf on Saturday and Sunday mornings. After a while, you begin to say, "They are not living many parts of their lives in common. Could it be that they aren't very well matched because they are so dissimilar?"

This list of similarities is different from the twenty-nine dimensions, although they will overlap in certain areas. Some items in the twenty-nine dimensions don't fall under the fifty similarities, and there are some helpful similarities, such as how money should be allocated for clothes, vacations, and other matters, that are not necessarily one of the matching dimensions. For instance, the socioeconomic backgrounds of your families should be considered. Let's say that your partner comes from a rather wealthy family, and you come from a very poor family. Is that a veto to your getting together?

Probably not. But let's say that you start stacking that difference on top of a difference in educational levels or verbal skills. One person likes to talk—and they are really good at it—and the other person is uncomfortable talking a lot, and is not good at it. When you begin to stack one dissimilarity on top of another, your chances of having a good marriage go down dramatically.

Attitude about weight is another area that it is important to have in common with your partner, but it is not one of the twenty-nine dimensions. If one person is constantly on a diet, trying to stay thin and trim, and the other person eats pretty much everything in sight and gains quite a bit of weight, that can be a dissimilarity that causes problems in a marriage.

Now, here's an interesting phenomenon that I've noticed. People who have a lot of similarities often don't even think about how harmonious their life is. They're too busy enjoying life! They just come home about the same time of day, eat their meals together—basically the same food at the same time, they like to watch the same things on television, they go to bed about the same time, and they get up at the same time, and they have the same love for their kids. They have the same set of interests or some overlapping interests. When someone asks, "How's your marriage?" they say, "Fine." They don't even realize that their marriage is great, because they have so many similarities.

On the other hand, people who have numerous dissimilarities notice them on a regular basis. When someone comes along and asks, "How is your marriage?" they say, "Well, it could be a whole lot better if she would . . ." or, "It could be a lot better if he stopped . . . ," and they have an entire list of dissimilarities they haven't yet worked through.

Think of it this way: Similarities are like assets in the bank, while dissimilarities with your partner are like debts you owe and will have to pay sooner or later. It is not devastating to have some debts as long as you have enough assets to cover them, but you certainly don't want so many debts that one unexpected event or added pressure will plunge you into relationship bankruptcy.

If a couple establishes a relationship or possibly even goes ahead and gets married, only to discover that they have too many dissimilarities, then what? Can you cultivate similarities, or can you work at being more similar? Yes, you can, but it takes time and patience. For instance, many things that Marylyn and I now have as similarities in our relationship started out as dissimilarities. For many years, I enjoyed popular music as well as musical comedy. Marylyn was from Boston, home of the famed Boston Symphony, and her dad raised her to love classical music. Before I met Marylyn, I regarded classical music as too dull and boring. *Who wants to listen to that stuff?* I'd say.

But then Marylyn introduced me to Mozart, Bach, Stravinsky, Beethoven, and many other great composers. Today, I love listening to Handel, Brahms, Chopin, Vivaldi, and many more. Because I have developed a taste for classical music, we have turned a dissimilarity into a similarity and eliminated a potential source of conflict. You can develop similarities over time if you are willing to move toward the other person. But if you can start your relationship with more in common, more similarities, life will be that much easier and more fulfilling.

I would like for singles to go through our fifty-item list of helpful marriage similarities with a potential relationship in mind. Mark each one, indicating that you and your partner are either similar or dissimilar in this regard. Carefully consider each item and ask yourself, *Which of these are crucial to me?* When you are finished, total up your similarities and your dissimilarities. If you match well on the twenty-nine dimensions and your similarities are in the high thirties to low forties, you probably have a relationship that will lead to a satisfying marriage. If you have less than that, well . . . let's just say, if you continue your relationship into marriage, it's going to take some serious negotiation, compromise, and work!

What we are trying to do is figure out what is important to you, and find somebody who is similar to you on that point. One of the best ways to do that is to specifically decide the top ten qualities that you must have in the love of your life, and ten things that you absolutely can't stand and would refuse to tolerate in marriage.

Your Must Haves and Can't Stands

Greg Forgatch and I wrote a little pamphlet called *How to Know If Someone Is Worth Pursuing in Two Dates or Less*. I was sitting at home one day, working on a book about that same subject, when I began mulling over things that a person must have in a mate. These things, of course, would not be the same for every person, so there were not "right" and "wrong" answers so much as points for each person to ponder.

Then I wondered, *If the "must haves" are the things I absolutely require in a potential partner, what are some of the things I could not possibly tolerate?* Out of those musings came a list of things I can't stand in a relationship. I quickly came up with twenty-five traits I must have, and twenty-five other traits I can't stand. Greg and Steve Carter suggested others, and we began collecting still more from a wide variety of sources. Before long, our list grew so long, we had to cut it back to make it manageable. Eventually we developed the fifty most popular "must haves" and the fifty least desirable "can't stands." We included on our list such "must haves" as:

- *Sense of Humor*: "I must have someone who is sharp and can enjoy the humorous side of life."
- *Passion*: "I must have someone who is willing to explore our sexual desires with passion and understanding."
- *Sociability*: "I must have a partner who loves to socialize with lots of different people."
- *Curiosity*: "I must have a partner who is hungry for new information and knowledge, and who strives to learn as much as possible."

Most people would agree with the statement "I must have a partner who is considered attractive by most current standards." But is it one of your top ten? How about "affection"? "I must have someone who is comfortable giving and receiving affection." Okay, is that one of your top ten? How about being "emotionally generous"?

If, for example, you like athletic contests either as a participant or as a spectator, in person or on television, you should not be matched with somebody who says, "Oh, sporting events! Why would you watch that?" If enjoying athletics is important to you, then you need to find someone who shares your interest in sports. For instance, our daughter Lorrie, who is married to Greg, always wanted to go to UCLA because of their great sports program. Greg attended USC, their cross-town rival. They both read the sports page every day and knew it almost by heart. They studied statistics and scores religiously, and they loved that in each other. Now they have four boys, and their boys are deeply involved in athletic contests. Does Lorrie like going to the games? She is the official scorekeeper! Does Greg like being there? He is the coach for all seasons! Their common love for sports helps to unite their family. For Greg and Lorrie, a love of sports would definitely be on their "must have" lists.

Once you establish your "must haves," you must do the same thing with your "can't stands." Pick the top ten (the traits you could tolerate the least in a mate). The "can't stands" include such traits as:

- *Vanity*: "I can't stand someone who is overly interested in his or her physical appearance."
- *Lying*: "I can't stand someone who lies to anyone—especially to me."
- *Depressed*: "I can't stand someone who is constantly unhappy about his or her life."
- *Mean-Spirited*: "I can't stand someone who has a devious nature and is mean to others."

Today on the eHarmony site, we have listed the fifty most popular "must haves" and the fifty most prevalent "can't stands." These are the qualities people have said are the most important criteria for them in choosing a marriage partner. From this list of fifty, we ask participants to create a list of their top ten "must haves" and their top ten "can't stands." This is an interesting exercise, but it takes some thinking to whittle the list down to only ten.

"But Dr. Warren, I feel like I am being so picky!" said Robyn. "Is that okay?"

It is more than okay; it is mandatory if you want to find your soul mate. If certain criteria matter to you, it is crucial that you find some-body who harmonizes with you in those areas. And the good news is, never in the history of the human race has it been so possible for you to be picky as a person who is looking for a lifetime partner. Thanks to sites such as eHarmony, you can afford to be picky about the things that matter most to you, because the field from which we are searching for your soul mate is much larger than simply the eligible singles in your hometown or in your social circles.

The fact is, it is not easy finding a person on your own who has every last thing you want, but with the help of modern technology, we may be able to find that person for you. That's why I want to em-phatically say: Don't marry anyone who doesn't have one of your top ten "must haves," or you will be frustrated a lot. That is an important point, so let's turn it around this way: Don't marry a person who doesn't have *all* of your top-ten "must haves." Similarly, don't marry a person who has *any* of your ten "can't stands."

"Wait a minute, Doc," I can almost hear you saying. "You must think I have a line of people outside my front door clear down the street from which to choose. And even if such a line existed, you act as though all of those people have all ten of my top ten must haves and none of my can't stands. But I only have this one guy, and he is hardly even interested in me."

Granted, you may not have a line of men or women who meet your high standards, but we might! There is no longer any need for you to limit yourself to the people you know, or recommendations by your friends, or people that you might meet at work or through other interactions in your local community. A whole world of men or women is literally at your fingertips. The Internet has allowed for enormous choice; you can get into a pool of candidates like ours where you have literally millions of potential partners from which to choose. With the proper matching systems such as we have at eHarmony, we can probably find someone who matches you in the twenty-nine dimensions as well as your "must haves" and "can't stands." You really have a chance to find somebody who has all ten of your must haves and none of your can't stands! And you can do it in a relatively expedient way.

Can you imagine how much time, energy, money spent on dead-end dates, and emotional frustration we can save you? More important, imagine the very real possibility of meeting your soul mate within the next twelve months! No wonder we say, "Who knew that science and love could be so compatible!"

APPENDIX B

Twenty Questions

To REALLY GET TO KNOW yourself, it's beneficial to discover how you think and feel about specific events and people that have helped shape your life. For each of these questions, write a brief paragraph to answer as honestly as possible; then ask a close friend or family member to evaluate your responses to see if you are missing any blind spots.

1. Who is the most important person in your life, and why?
2. What is the one dream for your life you most look forward to achieving?
3. Who has the capacity to make you angrier than anyone else in your life, and what in particular does he or she do to make you angry?
4. Who has the capacity to make you feel loved more than anyone else in your life, and what in particular does he or she do to cause you to feel so lovable?
5. What is it like being you? More precisely, how do you feel about yourself—physically, emotionally, mentally, and spiritually?
6. When do you feel inspired? Who and what contributes to your sense of inspiration? How does it feel when you are inspired?
7. What is the most important thing in the world to you?
8. If you had one day to live, how would you want to spend it?
9. When do you feel most afraid?

10. If you could accomplish only one thing during the rest of your life, what would it be?

11. What bores you? What always bores you, and what never bores you?

12. How important is money to you? How much time do you spend thinking about it, and what income level do you aspire to?

13. What is the role of God in your life? Do you believe there is a God, and if so, what is God like in relation to you?

14. In order, what are your three strongest interests?

15. Who is your biggest enemy, and precisely how and why did this person become your enemy?

16. How important is food to you? Do you think of it very often, and do you feel disciplined in your management of food intake?

17. Does the idea of being married to the same person for the rest of your life sound appealing to you—or not so appealing? What is there about it that you would especially like or not like?

18. Do you think of yourself as an emotionally healthy person? In what ways are you especially healthy, and in what ways could you use improvement?

19. What is the role of conflict in your life? Do you argue or fight very much with the people closest to you? How does it usually turn out?

20. What specifically would you like your closest friends to say about you at your funeral?

(Originally published on eHarmony.com. Subsequently published in Neil Clark Warren's *Date . . . Or Soul Mate?*; Nashville, TN: Thomas Nelson Publishers, 2002; pp. 31–34.)

APPENDIX C

Similarities or Differences?

YOUR SOUL MATE will most likely be someone who is a lot like you. As we've said throughout this book, opposites do attract, but for a lasting and satisfying relationship, you will do better if you and your partner have a lot of things in common. Below is a checklist of fifty items you can use to help you consider your similarities or differences. You'll notice that some of the categories on the checklist overlap the twenty-nine dimensions and others are distinct. While there is no perfect number of similarities a couple should have, I like to see at least thirty-five to forty similarities out of this list of fifty before a couple gets married.

As you go down through the list, you may want to mark an S for those areas in which you and your partner are similar, and a D for those in which you are different. Your totals will give you a fairly good idea of how similar you are to your partner . . . or how different the two of you are. Remember, your most satisfying relationship will be with someone who is a lot like you!

Check whether you are similar or different in each of the following areas:

1. Socio-economic background of family
2. Intelligence
3. Formal education
4. Verbal skills
5. Expected roles for both persons within the marriage
6. Views about power distribution within the family
7. Desired number of children

8. When a family should be started
9. Child-rearing views
10. Political philosophy
11. Views about smoking, alcohol, and drugs
12. Amount of involvement with in-laws
13. Sense of humor
14. Punctuality
15. Dependability
16. Desire for verbal intimacy and ability to be intimate
17. The role of conflict and how to resolve it
18. The way to handle anger
19. How friendships with the opposite sex should be handled
20. Expected amount of privacy and rules for its use
21. Level of ambition
22. Life goals
23. Attitudes about weight
24. Religious and spiritual beliefs and preferences
25. Amount of church involvement
26. Family spiritual involvement
27. Hobbies and interests
28. Type of music enjoyed
29. Energy level for physical activities
30. Sexual drive and sexual interest
31. Amount of income to be spent and saved
32. How money should be allocated (clothes, vacations, etc.)
33. Amount of money to be given away and to whom
34. Degree of risks to be taken with investments
35. Attitudes about cleanliness (house, clothes, body, etc.)
36. Ways of handling sickness
37. Health standards—when to see a doctor
38. Interpersonal and social skills
39. Amount and type of social involvement preferred
40. Geographical area in which to live
41. Size and style of house
42. Type of furniture and decorations
43. Amount and type of travel preferred

44. How to spend vacations
45. How to celebrate major holidays
46. How much time to spend together
47. When to go to sleep and get up
48. Temperature of home during the day and night
49. Activity during meals (talking, watching TV, etc.)
50. Television programs preferred

(Originally published as "50-Item List of Helpful Marriage Similarities" in Neil Clark Warren's *Finding the Love of Your Life*; Wheaton, IL: Tyndale House Publishers, 1992; pp. 60–61.)

HOW DID YOU DO? If you find that you are extremely different from your partner in your attitudes and desires, you would be unwise to allow your relationship to proceed beyond a friendship. Certainly some factors may change with time, but until they do, handle your relationship with that person cautiously.

On the other hand, if you have a large number of similarities with your partner, and you match well in the twenty-nine dimensions, you can have confidence that your relationship has a solid foundation, and if the chemistry between the two of you is good, you have the necessary ingredients for a strong, stable, and satisfying marriage.

HOW eHARMONY WORKS

OF ALL THE PEOPLE you meet in your life, only a few would make a great marriage partner for you. Some aren't attracted to you; others don't interest you. You may be highly compatible with someone, but the "chemistry" simply isn't there. Others aren't ready for a relationship. Many others may be great people with whom you might enjoy spending time, but they aren't compatible with you in the twenty-nine dimensions that make a great relationship, and are not potential marriage partners for you.

At eHarmony, we put our compatibility matching services to work for you, taking into full account the twenty-nine key dimensions that help predict compatibility and marital success. The results are matches unlike anything you will find anywhere else. The process may take longer, and cost a bit more than dating services, but eHarmony isn't about dating. Our goal is to help you find your soul mate!

Here's how it works:

1. WE FIND OUT ABOUT YOU.   You begin by going on-line at eHarmony.com and answering more than 500 questions based on the twenty-nine dimensions that our scientific research has shown are crucial to long-term success in relationships. Completing the survey is free, but it is hard work, and it takes some time and thought. The resulting profile empowers our matching system to find only the right matches for you among the millions of people on our site.

2. YOU LEARN ABOUT YOURSELF.   After completing our questionnaire, you will immediately receive your in-depth personality profile. Your

profile will show how you are seen by others and highlight your relationship strengths and weaknesses. This powerful tool will dramatically improve your odds for success in your next relationship.

3. WE FIND TRULY COMPATIBLE MATCHES FOR YOU.   The eHarmony matching model eliminates 99.7 percent of people who are *not* right for you, providing only matches who are truly compatible based on the twenty-nine key dimensions that predict relationship success as we've discussed in this book. With eHarmony doing all the hard work, you get to relax and concentrate on the chemistry of falling in love. You may not be attracted to every person with whom we match you, but you can be confident of this: If you honestly and accurately completed your questionnaire, we can find you matches who are a lot like you, and that is one of the key components to marital happiness.

4. YOU TAKE THE NEXT STEP—SAFELY AND RISK FREE.   When you are ready to take the next step and start communicating with one or more of your matches, you enroll as a member of eHarmony.com and choose a plan with which you are most comfortable—either a one-month plan, three months, six months, or one year. I encourage people to stay in the system longer for two reasons (neither of which has anything to do with money): one, by staying in the system longer, you reduce the pressure on yourself to find somebody quickly. Take your time. The right person is out there; let us help you find the perfect soul mate for you! Second, remember that each day approximately ten thousand *new* people are signing on to eHarmony.com. Your soul mate may be one of them. If we haven't found the right person for you yet, don't give up. It is literally only a matter of time. Besides, eHarmony has a money-back guarantee. If we can't find you matches, we will extend your membership for free or refund your money. One date could cost you anywhere from fifty to a hundred to two hundred dollars or more. You can save a lot of time and money by allowing eHarmony to match you with people that we know are compatible with you.

5. YOU LEARN ABOUT YOUR MATCHES IN DEPTH. Okay, you've made the decision to check out your matches. We'll help you to do so safely and wisely, without compromising your privacy (or your dignity), or giving too much information too soon. It's time to ask the important questions *before* you get too involved, so there are no surprises later. We'll help you communicate with your matches safely and discreetly. We'll provide you with tough questions to ask your matches; you can share your "must haves" and "can't stands," and exchange photos when *you* are ready to do so.

We'll walk with you through four stages of guided communication, e-mailing each other through eHarmony's safe, anonymous message system until you are ready to share your personal information. If that doesn't occur, we'll help by blocking further communication from people you no longer wish to hear from.

Stage one: We'll start by helping you to "break the ice." Just saying hello is often the hardest part of meeting someone new. At eHarmony, we help you establish contact and start the conversations. When you let us know that you are interested in one of your matches, we contact that person with an e-mail message such as "Neil, from Pasadena would like to communicate with you." Although you can be sure that you and Neil are compatible, we provide you with some basic information about Neil, and you decide if you'd like to hear from him or not. If you say "No," that's that. We respond to Neil, informing him that you have chosen not to respond at this time. If you agree to hear from Neil, you'll choose five multiple choice questions to ask your match that will help you build a rapport and let you begin to get to know that person. At the same time, you'll share some of the things that are important to you.

Stage two: Next, we'll help you determine what is important (after reading this book, you should have a fairly good idea of that!). We'll help you to make up your list of "Must Haves" and "Can't Stands" and then prompt you to ask some important questions and exchange answers with your match to see how your lists compare.

Stage three: Asking deeper questions is hard, but important. So, in this stage of communication, we will help you communicate through short paragraphs of information. As you get to know each other, eHarmony will help you write and exchange questions that explore issues people often overlook in their relationships until it's too late.

Stage four: When you feel comfortable with the person with whom you have been communicating, eHarmony helps you move to "open communication," still within the eHarmony system to help safeguard your relationship, and to help you should problems occur. If you move to open communication and then decide that this person is not for you, no problem. You can limit or close communication completely, and begin the process with someone else. While some people find their soul mate on the first match, many others communicate with dozens before finding their perfect match. There's no rush and no extra charge for communicating with more of your matches.

At any point, if you prefer, you can move directly to completely open communication—outside of eHarmony's purview—and engage in communication with someone with whom you have been matched. You are in control; you make the calls. We encourage you, however, to take your time, to explore and analyze carefully the information you receive, and to fall in love for all the right reasons!

(This information adapted from the eHarmony.com site. Copyright © 2004 eHarmony.com)